It's another Quality Book from CGP

This book is for anyone doing GCSE Biology.

First we take all the really important stuff
you need to pass GCSE Biology —
and we stick it in a book.
Then we have a real good stab at trying
to make it funny — so you'll actually use it.
Simple as that.

What CGP is all about

Our sole aim here at CGP is to produce the highest quality
books — carefully written, immaculately presented, and
dangerously close to being funny.

Then we work our socks off to get them out to you
— at the cheapest possible prices.

Contents

Page References for Modular Syllabuses

NEAB Double Award Science — Modular Syllabus

EdExel Double Award Science — Modular Syllabus

                    (The rest of this module is covered in the Physics Book.)

SEG Double Award Science — Modular Syllabus

                    (A little of this module is covered in the Chemistry Book.)

We also do the best Syllabus-Specific Revision Guides you can buy

In addition to our usual KS4 science revision guides (like this one), we also produce brilliant syllabus-specific versions for the NEAB and SEG syllabuses.

These are just the same except the content has been tweaked to exactly match each particular syllabus. And don't forget, unlike other people's boring books, ours always have lots of ridiculous jokes in them. Please phone for details — see inside front cover.

Published by Coordination Group Publications Ltd.

Illustrations by: Sandy Gardner, e-mail: illustrations@sandygardner.co.uk
                    and Bowser, Colorado USA.

ISBN   1 841 146 601 8

Groovy website: www.cgpbooks.co.uk

Printed by Elanders Hindson, Newcastle upon Tyne.
Clipart sources: CorelDRAW and VECTOR.

1001

Life Processes and Cells

The Seven Life Processes which show you're alive

There are seven things they call "*LIFE PROCESSES*", — things that *all plants and animals do*.
You should learn all seven well enough to write them down *from memory*.
Use the little jollyism "MRS NERG" to remind you of the first letter of each word.

M — Movement	Being able to *move* parts of the body.
R — Reproduction	Producing *offspring*.
S — Sensitivity	*Responding* to the outside world.
N — Nutrition	Getting *food* in where it's needed.
E — Excretion	*Getting rid* of waste products.
R — Respiration	Turning *food into energy*.
G — Growth	Getting to *adult size*.

(If you think about it, this list describes the entire life of a sheep — and a frighteningly large chunk of yours too.)

Plant Cells and Animal Cells Have Their Differences

You need to be able to draw these two cells *WITH ALL THE DETAILS* for each.

Animal Cell

Plant Cell

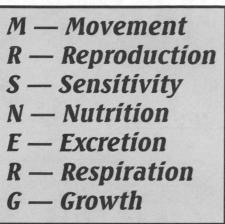

4 THINGS THEY BOTH HAVE IN COMMON:

1) *NUCLEUS* controls what the cell *does*.

2) *CYTOPLASM* where the *chemical reactions* happen.

3) *CELL MEMBRANE* holds the cell together and *controls* what goes *in and out*.

4) *MITOCHONDRIA* turn glucose and oxygen into *energy*.

3 EXTRAS THAT ONLY THE PLANT CELL HAS:

1) *RIGID CELL WALL* made of *cellulose*, gives *support* for the cell.

2) *VACUOLE* Contains *cell sap*, a weak solution of sugar and salts.

3) *GREEN CHLOROPLASTS* containing *chlorophyll* for *photosynthesis*.

Have you learnt it? — let's see, shall we...

Right then, when you're ready, when you think you've learnt it, *cover the page* and *answer these*:
1) What are the 7 life processes, and what's the little jolly for remembering them?
2) Draw an animal cell and a plant cell and put all the labels on them.
3) What 4 things do plant and animal cells have in common?
4) What are the 3 differences between them?

Specialised Plant Cells

Most cells are _SPECIALISED_ for a specific job, and in the Exam you'll probably have to explain why the cell they've shown you is so good at its job. It's a lot easier if you've _already learnt them_!

1) Palisade Leaf Cells are Designed for Photosynthesis

1) Packed with _chloroplasts_ for _photosynthesis_.
2) _Tall shape_ means a lot of _surface area_ exposed down the side for _absorbing_ CO_2 from the air in the leaf.
3) Tall shape also means a good chance of _light_ hitting a _chloroplast_ before it reaches the bottom of the cell.

2) Guard Cells are Designed to Open and Close

1) Special _kidney shape_ which _opens and closes_ the stomata (a single pore is a stoma) as the cells go _turgid_ or _flaccid_.
2) _Thin_ outer walls and _thickened_ inner walls make this opening and closing function work properly.
3) They're also _sensitive to light_ and _close at night_ to conserve water without losing out on photosynthesis.

3) Three Other Important Examples:

There are three other important examples of specialised plant cells: _Root Hair cells_ (P. 4), _Phloem cells_ (P. 9) and _Xylem tubes_ (P. 9). Look them up and see how they're specialised.

Cells, Tissues, Organs and Organ Systems

They like asking this in Exams, so learn the sequence:

> A group of _**SIMILAR CELLS**_ is called a _**TISSUE**_.
> A group of _**DIFFERENT TISSUES**_ form an _**ORGAN**_.
> A _**GROUP OF ORGANS**_ working together form an _**ORGAN SYSTEM**_, or even _**A WHOLE ORGANISM**_.

(This can apply to animals as well as plants, of course.)

A JOLLY EXAMPLE:

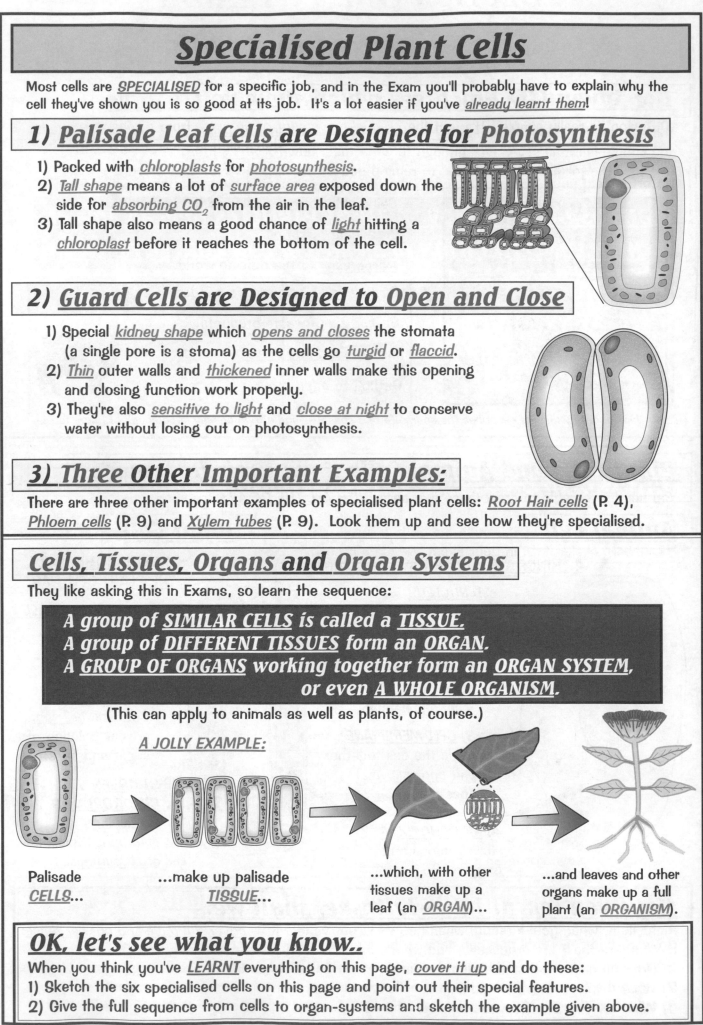

Palisade _CELLS_...

...make up palisade _TISSUE_...

...which, with other tissues make up a leaf (an _ORGAN_)...

...and leaves and other organs make up a full plant (an _ORGANISM_).

OK, let's see what you know..

When you think you've _LEARNT_ everything on this page, _cover it up_ and do these:
1) Sketch the six specialised cells on this page and point out their special features.
2) Give the full sequence from cells to organ-systems and sketch the example given above.

Diffusion

Don't be put off by the fancy word

"Diffusion" is really simple. It's just the _gradual movement of particles_ from _places where there are lots of them_ to places where there are _less of them_. That's all it is — _IT'S JUST THE NATURAL TENDENCY FOR STUFF TO SPREAD OUT_.

Unfortunately you also have to _LEARN_ the fancy way of saying the same thing, which is this:

DIFFUSION is the MOVEMENT OF PARTICLES from an area of HIGH CONCENTRATION to an area of LOW CONCENTRATION

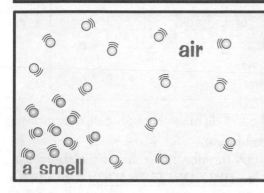

air

a smell

smell diffused in the air

Diffusion of Gases in Leaves is vital for Photosynthesis

The _simplest type_ of diffusion is where _different gases diffuse through each other_, like when a weird smell spreads out through the air in a room. Diffusion of gases also happens in _leaves_ and they'll very likely put it in your Exam. _So learn it now_:

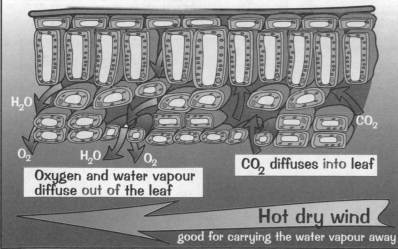

H_2O

O_2 H_2O O_2

Oxygen and water vapour diffuse out of the leaf

CO_2

CO_2 diffuses into leaf

Hot dry wind
good for carrying the water vapour away

For _PHOTOSYNTHESIS_ to happen, _carbon dioxide_ gas has to get _inside the leaves_.

It does this by DIFFUSION through the biddy little holes under the leaf called _stomata_.

At the same time _water vapour_ and _oxygen_ diffuse _out_ through the same biddy little holes.

The water vapour escapes by _diffusion_ because _there's a lot of it inside the leaf_ and _less of it in the air outside_. _This diffusion causes TRANSPIRATION and it goes quicker_ when the air around the leaf is kept _DRY_ — i.e. transpiration is quickest in _HOT, DRY, WINDY CONDITIONS_ — and don't you forget it!

So, how much do you know about diffusion?

Yeah sure it's a pretty book but actually the big idea is to _learn_ all the stuff that's in it.

So learn this page until you can answer these questions _without having to look back_:

1) Write down the fancy definition for diffusion, and then say what it means in your own words.
2) Draw the cross-section of the leaf with arrows to show which way the three gases diffuse.
3) What weather conditions make the diffusion of water vapour out of the leaf go fastest?

Diffusion Through Cell Membranes

Cell membranes are kind of clever...

They're kind of clever because they hold everything _inside_ the cell, _BUT_, they let stuff _in and out_ as well.   Only very _small molecules_ can diffuse through cell membranes though — things like _glucose_ or _amino acids_.

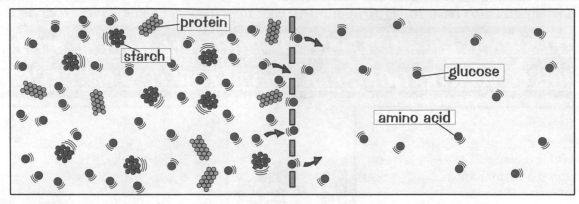

1) Notice that _BIG MOLECULES_ like _STARCH_ or _PROTEINS_ can't diffuse through cell membranes — they could quite cheerfully ask you exactly that in the Exam.
2) Just like with diffusion in air, particles flow through the cell membrane from where there's a _HIGH CONCENTRATION_ (a lot of them) to where there's a _LOW CONCENTRATION_ (not such a lot of them).

Root Hairs take in Minerals using Active Uptake

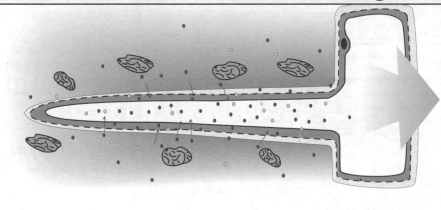

Root Hair cell

1) The cells on plant roots grow into long "_hairs_" which stick out into the soil.

2) This gives the plant a _big surface area_ for absorbing _water and minerals_ from the soil.

3) The concentration of minerals is _higher_ in the _root hair_ cell than in the _soil_ around it.
4) So normal diffusion _doesn't_ explain how minerals are _taken up_ into the root hair cell.
5) They should go _the other way_ if they followed the rules of _diffusion_.
6) The answer is that a conveniently mysterious process called "_active uptake_" is responsible.
7) _Active uptake_ allows the plant to absorb minerals _against the concentration gradient_. This is essential for its growth. But active uptake _needs energy_ from the plant to make it work.
8) _Active uptake_ also happens in _humans_, in taking _glucose_ from the _gut_ and _kidney tubules_ (P. 49).

A Real Easy Page to Learn...

Make sure you can do these with the page covered up — if you can't, you ain't learnt nothin':
1) What type of molecules _will_ diffuse through cell membranes and what type _won't_?
2) Give two examples of each.
3) Draw a full diagram of a root hair and say what it does.

Osmosis

Osmosis is a Special Case of Diffusion, that's all

> **OSMOSIS** is the _movement of water molecules_ across a _partially permeable membrane_ from a region of **HIGH WATER CONCENTRATION** to a region of **LOW WATER CONCENTRATION**.

1) A _partially permeable membrane_ is just one with _real small holes_ in it. So small, in fact, that _only water molecules_ can pass through them, and bigger molecules like _glucose_ can't.

2) _Visking tubing_ is a partially permeable membrane that you should learn the _name_ of. It's also called _dialysis tubing_ because it's used in _kidney dialysis machines_.

3) The water molecules actually pass _both ways_ through the membrane in a _two-way traffic_.

4) But because there are _more on one side_ than the other there's a steady _net flow_ into the region with _fewer_ water molecules, i.e. into the _stronger solution_ (of glucose).

5) This causes the _glucose-rich_ region to _fill up with water_. The water acts like it's trying to _dilute_ it, so as to "_even up_" the concentration either side of the membrane.

6) _OSMOSIS_ makes _plant_ cells _swell up_ if they're surrounded by _weak solution_ and they become _TURGID_. This is real useful for giving _support_ to green plant tissue and for _opening stomatal guard cells_.

7) _Animal_ cells _don't have a cell wall_ and can easily _burst_ if put into pure water because they _take in_ so much water _by osmosis_.

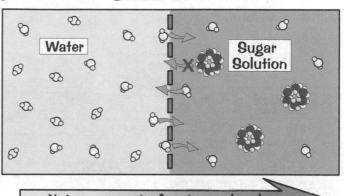

Net movement of water molecules

Turgid plant cell   Animal cell bursting

Two Osmosis Experiments — Favourites for the Exams

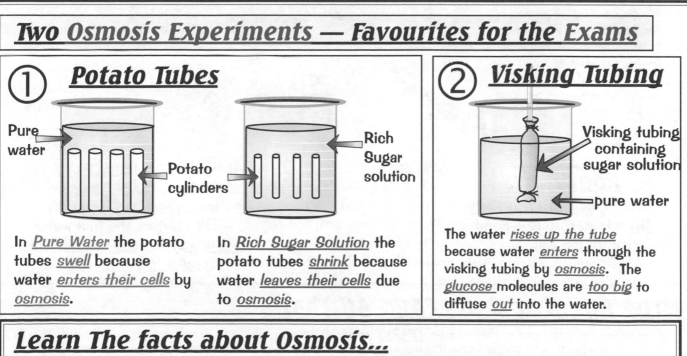

① Potato Tubes

Pure water

Potato cylinders

Rich Sugar solution

In _Pure Water_ the potato tubes _swell_ because water _enters their cells_ by _osmosis_.

In _Rich Sugar Solution_ the potato tubes _shrink_ because water _leaves their cells_ due to _osmosis_.

② Visking Tubing

Visking tubing containing sugar solution

pure water

The water _rises up the tube_ because water _enters_ through the visking tubing by _osmosis_. The _glucose_ molecules are _too big_ to diffuse _out_ into the water.

Learn The facts about Osmosis...

Osmosis can be kind of confusing if you don't get to the bottom of it. In normal diffusion, glucose molecules move, but with small enough holes they can't. That's when only water moves through the membrane, and then it's called _osmosis_. Easy peasy, I'd say. _Learn and enjoy_.

Basic Plant Structure

You have to know all these parts of the plant and what they do:

The Five Different Bits of a Plant all do Different Jobs

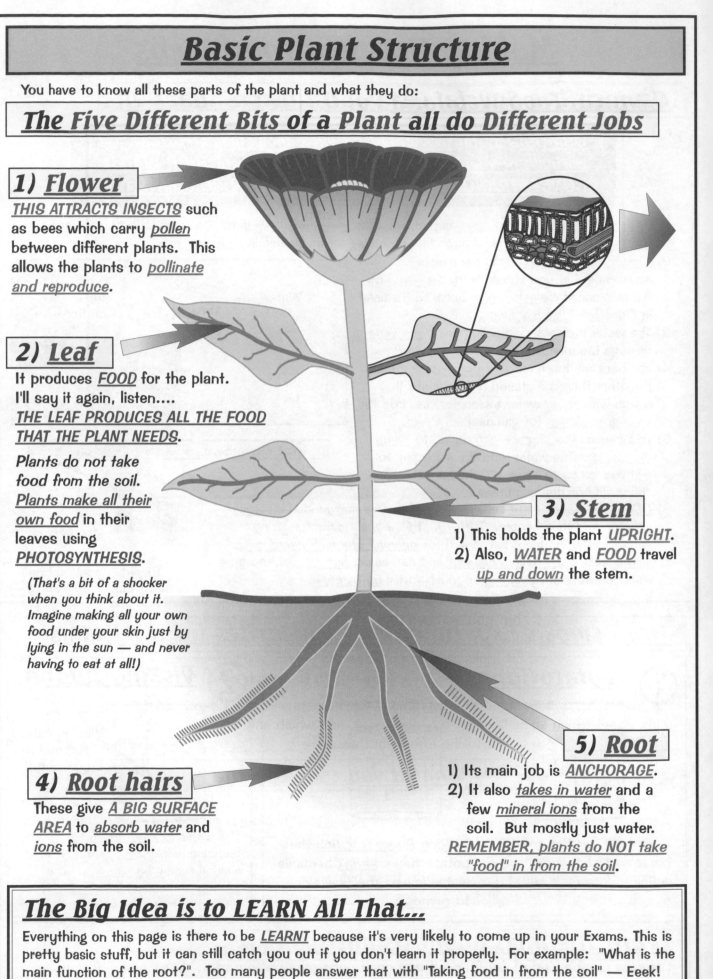

1) Flower

THIS ATTRACTS INSECTS such as bees which carry *pollen* between different plants. This allows the plants to *pollinate and reproduce.*

2) Leaf

It produces *FOOD* for the plant. I'll say it again, listen....
THE LEAF PRODUCES ALL THE FOOD THAT THE PLANT NEEDS.

Plants do not take food from the soil. *Plants make all their own food* in their leaves using *PHOTOSYNTHESIS.*

(That's a bit of a shocker when you think about it. Imagine making all your own food under your skin just by lying in the sun — and never having to eat at all!)

3) Stem

1) This holds the plant *UPRIGHT*.
2) Also, *WATER* and *FOOD* travel *up and down* the stem.

5) Root

1) Its main job is *ANCHORAGE*.
2) It also *takes in water* and a few *mineral ions* from the soil. But mostly just water.
REMEMBER, plants do NOT take "food" in from the soil.

4) Root hairs

These give *A BIG SURFACE AREA* to *absorb water* and *ions* from the soil.

The Big Idea is to LEARN All That...

Everything on this page is there to be *LEARNT* because it's very likely to come up in your Exams. This is pretty basic stuff, but it can still catch you out if you don't learn it properly. For example: "What is the main function of the root?". Too many people answer that with "Taking food in from the soil" — Eeek! LEARN these facts. They all count. They're all worth marks in the Exam. Practise until you can sketch the diagram and scribble down *ALL* the details, *without looking back*.

SECTION ONE — PLANTS

Leaf Structure

Leaves are Designed for One Thing Only...
— Making Food by Photosynthesis

The whole structure of leaves is geared towards that. Make sure you learn this diagram with all its labels:

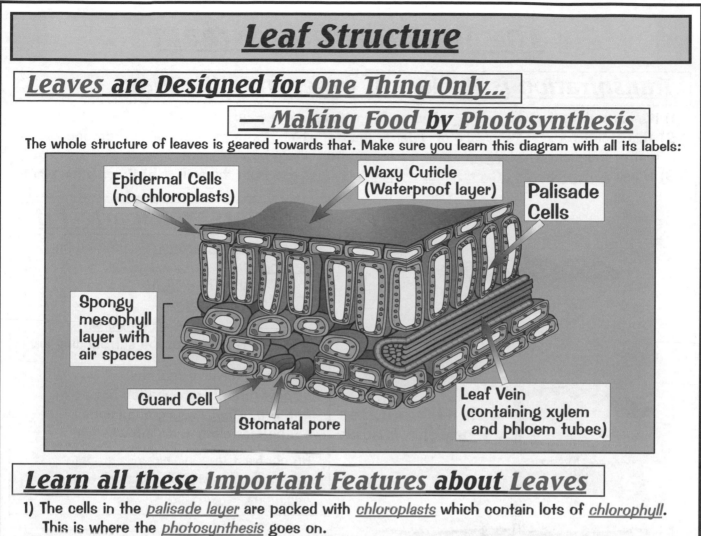

Epidermal Cells (no chloroplasts)

Waxy Cuticle (Waterproof layer)

Palisade Cells

Spongy mesophyll layer with air spaces

Guard Cell

Stomatal pore

Leaf Vein (containing xylem and phloem tubes)

Learn all these Important Features about Leaves

1) The cells in the _palisade layer_ are packed with _chloroplasts_ which contain lots of _chlorophyll_. This is where the _photosynthesis_ goes on.

2) The _palisade_ and _spongy layers_ are full of _air spaces_ to allow CO_2 to reach the palisade cells.

3) The cells in the _epidermis_ make _wax_ which covers the _leaf surface_, especially the _top surface_. This is to _prevent water loss_.

4) The _lower surface_ is full of biddy little holes called _stomata_. They are there to _let CO_2 in_. They also allow water to escape — this is how the _transpiration stream_ comes about.

5) _Xylem_ and _phloem_ vessels cover the whole leaf like tiny '_veins_', to _deliver water_ to every part of the leaf and then to _take away the food_ (starch) produced by the leaf.

Stomata are Pores which Open and Close Automatically

1) _Stomata_ close _automatically_ when supplies of water from the roots start to _dry up_.

2) The _guard cells_ control this. When water is _scarce_, they become _flaccid_, and they change shape, which _closes_ the stomatal pores.

3) This _prevents_ any more water being _lost_, but also stops CO_2 getting in, so the photosynthesis stops as well.

Cells _TURGID_, pore _OPENS_

Cells _FLACCID_, pore _CLOSES_

Spend some time poring over these facts...

Two spiffing diagrams and a few simple features. What could be easier? Check the clock and give yourself five minutes of intense active learning to see how much you can learn. "_Intense active learning_" means _covering the page_ and _scribbling down_ the details, but don't take 5 minutes drawing out a neat diagram of a leaf — that's just a waste of precious time.

8

The Transpiration Stream

Transpiration is the loss of water from the Plant

1) It's caused by the _evaporation_ of water from _inside the leaves_.
2) This creates a _slight shortage_ of water in the leaf which _draws more water up_ from the rest of the plant which _in turn_ draws more up from the _roots_.
3) It has _two beneficial effects_: a) _it transports minerals_ from the soil   b) it _cools_ the plant.

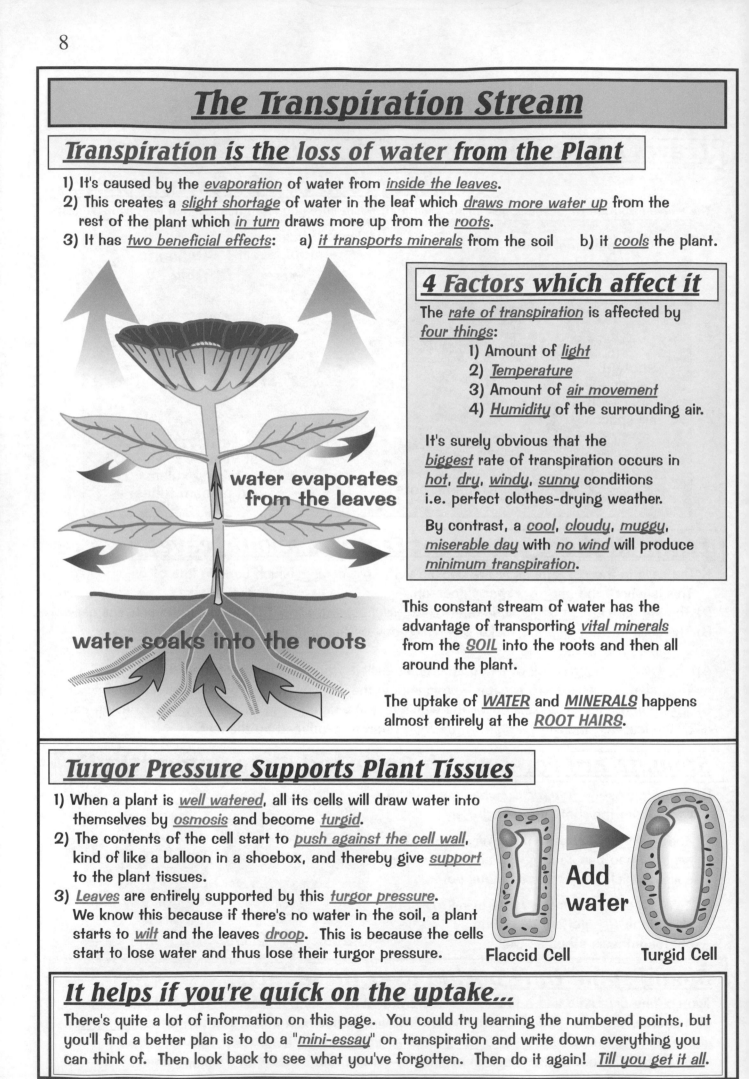

water evaporates from the leaves

water soaks into the roots

4 Factors which affect it

The _rate of transpiration_ is affected by _four things_:
   1) Amount of _light_
   2) _Temperature_
   3) Amount of _air movement_
   4) _Humidity_ of the surrounding air.

It's surely obvious that the _biggest_ rate of transpiration occurs in _hot_, _dry_, _windy_, _sunny_ conditions i.e. perfect clothes-drying weather.

By contrast, a _cool_, _cloudy_, _muggy_, _miserable day_ with _no wind_ will produce _minimum transpiration_.

This constant stream of water has the advantage of transporting _vital minerals_ from the _SOIL_ into the roots and then all around the plant.

The uptake of _WATER_ and _MINERALS_ happens almost entirely at the _ROOT HAIRS_.

Turgor Pressure Supports Plant Tissues

1) When a plant is _well watered_, all its cells will draw water into themselves by _osmosis_ and become _turgid_.
2) The contents of the cell start to _push against the cell wall_, kind of like a balloon in a shoebox, and thereby give _support_ to the plant tissues.
3) _Leaves_ are entirely supported by this _turgor pressure_. We know this because if there's no water in the soil, a plant starts to _wilt_ and the leaves _droop_. This is because the cells start to lose water and thus lose their turgor pressure.

Add water

Flaccid Cell   Turgid Cell

It helps if you're quick on the uptake...

There's quite a lot of information on this page. You could try learning the numbered points, but you'll find a better plan is to do a "_mini-essay_" on transpiration and write down everything you can think of. Then look back to see what you've forgotten. Then do it again! _Till you get it all_.

Transport Systems in Plants

Plants need to transport various things around inside themselves. They have tubes for it.

Phloem and Xylem Vessels Transport Different Things

1) Plants have _two separate sets of tubes_ for transporting stuff around the plant.
2) _Both_ sets of tubes go to _every part of the plant_, but they are totally _separate_.
3) They usually run _alongside_ each other.

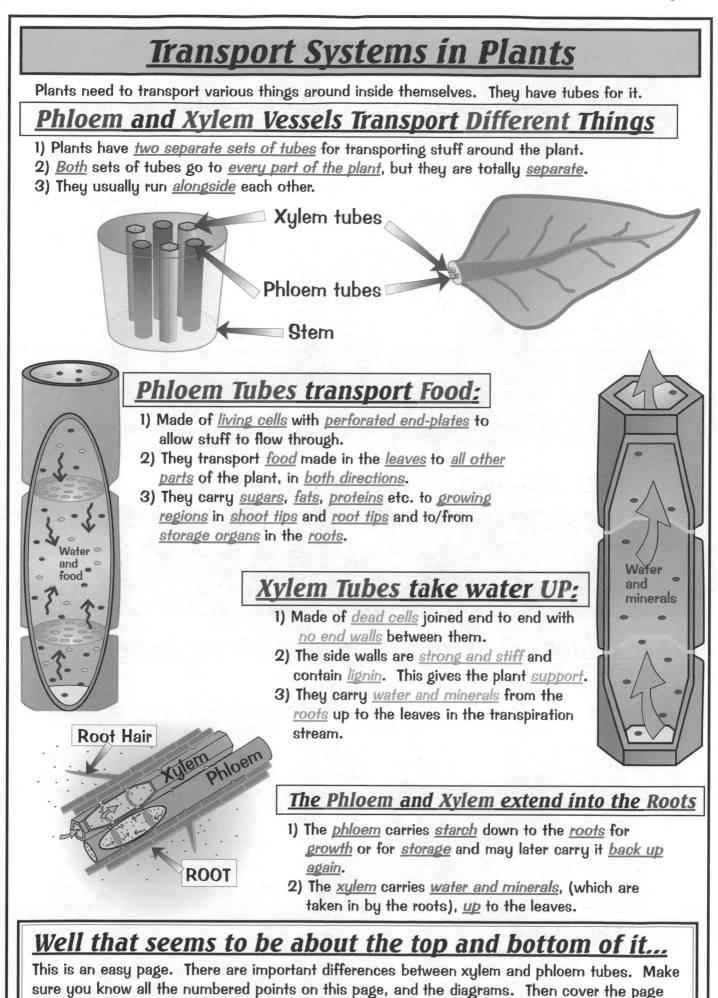

Xylem tubes

Phloem tubes

Stem

Phloem Tubes transport Food:

1) Made of _living cells_ with _perforated end-plates_ to allow stuff to flow through.
2) They transport _food_ made in the _leaves_ to _all other parts_ of the plant, in _both directions_.
3) They carry _sugars_, _fats_, _proteins_ etc. to _growing regions_ in _shoot tips_ and _root tips_ and to/from _storage organs_ in the _roots_.

Water and food

Xylem Tubes take water UP:

1) Made of _dead cells_ joined end to end with _no end walls_ between them.
2) The side walls are _strong and stiff_ and contain _lignin_. This gives the plant _support_.
3) They carry _water and minerals_ from the _roots_ up to the leaves in the transpiration stream.

Water and minerals

Root Hair

Xylem

Phloem

ROOT

The Phloem and Xylem extend into the Roots

1) The _phloem_ carries _starch_ down to the _roots_ for _growth_ or for _storage_ and may later carry it _back up again_.
2) The _xylem_ carries _water and minerals_, (which are taken in by the roots), _up_ to the leaves.

Well that seems to be about the top and bottom of it...

This is an easy page. There are important differences between xylem and phloem tubes. Make sure you know all the numbered points on this page, and the diagrams. Then cover the page and scribble it all down with detailed sketches of the diagrams. Then do it again, _until you get it all_.

Photosynthesis

Photosynthesis Produces Glucose from Sunlight

1) _Photosynthesis_ is the process that _produces 'food'_ in plants. The 'food' it produces is _glucose_.
2) Photosynthesis _takes place_ in the _leaves_ of all _green plants_ — this is what leaves _are for_.

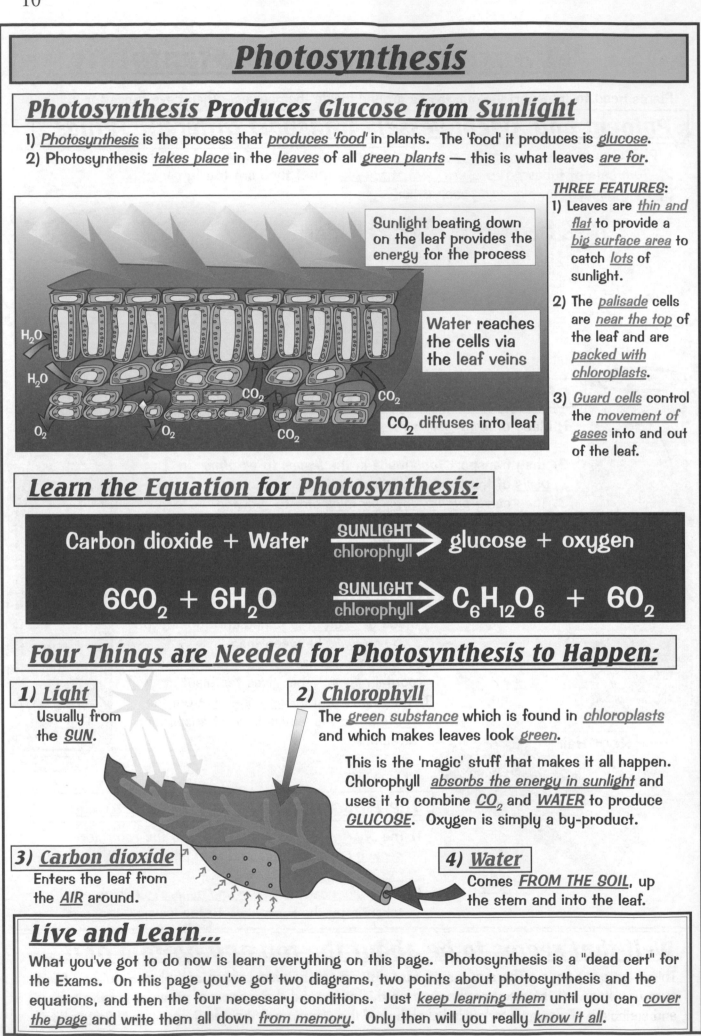

Sunlight beating down on the leaf provides the energy for the process

Water reaches the cells via the leaf veins

CO_2 diffuses into leaf

H_2O

H_2O

O_2

O_2

CO_2

CO_2

CO_2

THREE FEATURES:

1) Leaves are _thin and flat_ to provide a _big surface area_ to catch _lots_ of sunlight.

2) The _palisade_ cells are _near the top_ of the leaf and are _packed with chloroplasts_.

3) _Guard cells_ control the _movement of gases_ into and out of the leaf.

Learn the Equation for Photosynthesis:

Carbon dioxide + Water $\xrightarrow[\text{chlorophyll}]{\text{SUNLIGHT}}$ glucose + oxygen

$$6CO_2 + 6H_2O \xrightarrow[\text{chlorophyll}]{\text{SUNLIGHT}} C_6H_{12}O_6 + 6O_2$$

Four Things are Needed for Photosynthesis to Happen:

1) Light
Usually from the _SUN_.

2) Chlorophyll
The _green substance_ which is found in _chloroplasts_ and which makes leaves look _green_.

This is the 'magic' stuff that makes it all happen. Chlorophyll _absorbs the energy in sunlight_ and uses it to combine _CO_2_ and _WATER_ to produce _GLUCOSE_. Oxygen is simply a by-product.

3) Carbon dioxide
Enters the leaf from the _AIR_ around.

4) Water
Comes _FROM THE SOIL_, up the stem and into the leaf.

Live and Learn...

What you've got to do now is learn everything on this page. Photosynthesis is a "dead cert" for the Exams. On this page you've got two diagrams, two points about photosynthesis and the equations, and then the four necessary conditions. Just _keep learning them_ until you can _cover the page_ and write them all down _from memory_. Only then will you really _know it all_.

SECTION ONE — PLANTS

Altering the Rate of Photosynthesis

The _RATE_ of _photosynthesis_ is affected by _THREE FACTORS_:

1) THE AMOUNT OF LIGHT (and the wavelength)

The _chlorophyll_ uses _light energy_ to perform photosynthesis. It can only do it as fast as the light energy is arriving. Chlorophyll actually only absorbs the _red_ and _blue_ ends of the _visible light spectrum_, but not the _green light_ in the middle, which is _reflected_ back. This is why the plant looks green.

2) THE AMOUNT OF CARBON DIOXIDE

CO_2 and _water_ are the _raw materials_. Water is never really in short supply in a plant but only _0.03%_ of the air around is CO_2 so it's actually _pretty scarce_ as far as plants are concerned.

3) THE TEMPERATURE

Chlorophyll is like an _ENZYME_ in that it works best when it's _warm but not too hot_. The rate of photosynthesis depends on how 'happy' the chlorophyll enzyme is: _WARM_ but not too hot.

Three Important Graphs For Rate of Photosynthesis

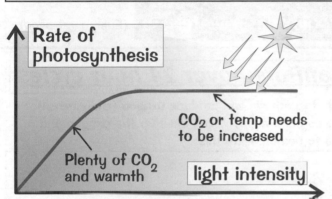

At any given time one or other of the above _three factors_ will be the _limiting factor_ which is keeping the photosynthesis _down_ at the rate it is.

1) If the _light level_ is raised, the rate of photosynthesis will _increase steadily_ but only up to a _certain point_.

2) Beyond that, it won't make any _difference_ because then it'll be either the _temperature_ or the CO_2 level which is wrong and which is now the limiting factor.

3) Conversely, if the _light level_ is too _low_, then changing the amount of CO_2 _won't_ increase the rate of photosynthesis at all — _not until_ the light level is _raised_ to _match_ the CO_2 level.

4) To get _optimum rate_ of photosynthesis you need to make sure that
   1) There's _enough CO_2_
   2) There's _plenty of light_
   3) The _temperature_ is just right

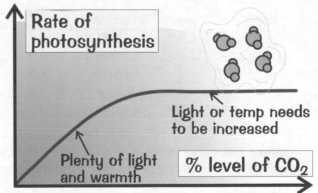

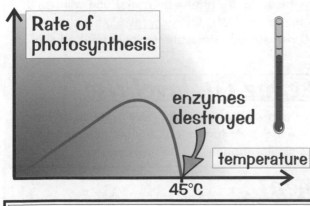

5) Note that you can't really have _too much_ light or CO_2. The _temperature_ however must _not_ get too high or it _destroys_ the chlorophyll enzymes.

6) This happens at about 45°C (which is pretty hot for outdoors, though greenhouses can get that hot if you're not careful).

7) _Usually_, though, if the temperature is the _limiting factor_ it's because it's too low, and things need _warming up a bit_.

Revision — life isn't all fun and sunshine...

There are three limiting factors, a graph for each and an explanation of why the graphs level off or stop abruptly. _Cover the page_ and practise _recalling all these details_, until you can do it.

Photosynthesis and Respiration

Photosynthesis and Respiration are OPPOSITE Processes:

1) Remember that _photosynthesis in plants_ provides the _food_ for _all animals_.
   Plants _trap the Sun's energy_ and turn it into _glucose_, which is basically _stored chemical energy_. Animals along the _food chain_ then use that energy in _respiration_ to live and grow. Without plants, all animals would _die_.

2) Respiration _uses up oxygen and glucose_ and turns it back into _carbon dioxide_ and _water_.

The EQUATIONS are the same but in opposite directions:

Photosynthesis:
   carbon dioxide + water → glucose + oxygen   (_Requires_ Energy)

Respiration:
   glucose + oxygen → carbon dioxide + water   (Energy _released_)

Enclosed Plants: O_2 and CO_2 monitored over 24 hour cycles

In daylight (or any other light, except _green_) plants do photosynthesis and produce oxygen (and glucose). But both plants and animals do respiration all the time, day and night, which uses up the oxygen and releases carbon dioxide. An experiment can be done to demonstrate this:

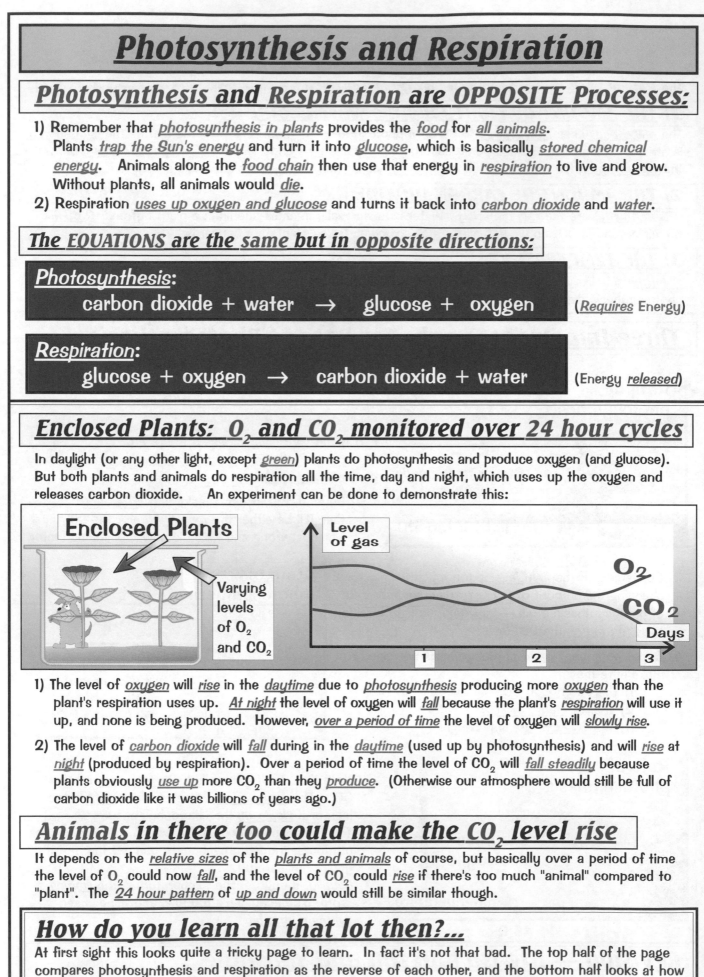

1) The level of _oxygen_ will _rise_ in the _daytime_ due to _photosynthesis_ producing more _oxygen_ than the plant's respiration uses up. _At night_ the level of oxygen will _fall_ because the plant's _respiration_ will use it up, and none is being produced. However, _over a period of time_ the level of oxygen will _slowly rise_.

2) The level of _carbon dioxide_ will _fall_ during in the _daytime_ (used up by photosynthesis) and will _rise_ at _night_ (produced by respiration). Over a period of time the level of CO_2 will _fall steadily_ because plants obviously _use up_ more CO_2 than they _produce_. (Otherwise our atmosphere would still be full of carbon dioxide like it was billions of years ago.)

Animals _in there_ too could make the CO_2 level rise

It depends on the _relative sizes_ of the _plants and animals_ of course, but basically over a period of time the level of O_2 could now _fall_, and the level of CO_2 could _rise_ if there's too much "animal" compared to "plant". The _24 hour pattern_ of _up and down_ would still be similar though.

How do you learn all that lot then?...

At first sight this looks quite a tricky page to learn. In fact it's not that bad. The top half of the page compares photosynthesis and respiration as the reverse of each other, and the bottom half looks at how the levels of oxygen and CO_2 vary over periods of 24 hours or longer. With that basic structure in mind you can _cover the page_ and try to _scribble it all down_. It's really not that difficult.

Two Leaf Experiments

There are two particularly jolly leaf experiments which they're quite likely to test in your Exams:

1) Photosynthesis and the Starch Test
(Another sixties pop group — or maybe not.)

1) This is a _real simple experiment_ to find out what affects _starch production_ (and therefore _photosynthesis_) in a leaf. (The answer is, of course _light_ and _carbon dioxide_.)

2) All the experiment does is _deprive_ parts of a leaf of either _light_ or _carbon dioxide_ for 24 hours or so and then _test for starch_ using _iodine_.

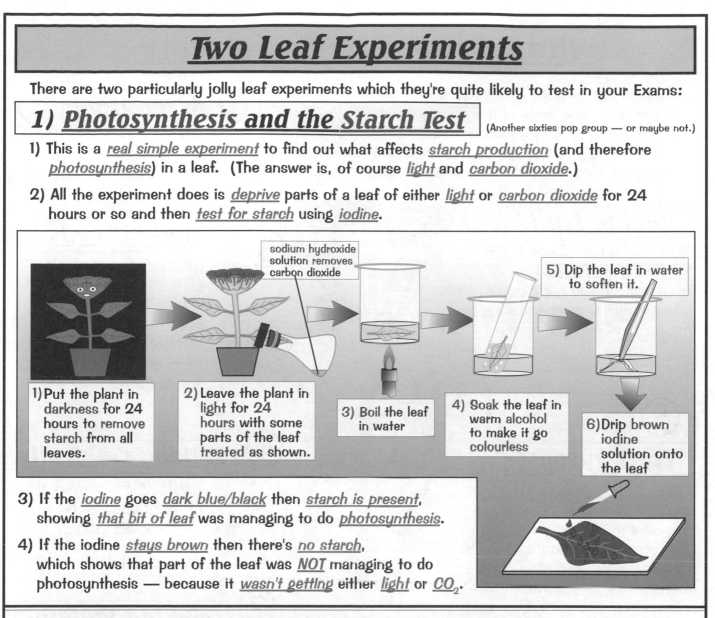

sodium hydroxide solution removes carbon dioxide

5) Dip the leaf in water to soften it.

1) Put the plant in darkness for 24 hours to remove starch from all leaves.

2) Leave the plant in light for 24 hours with some parts of the leaf treated as shown.

3) Boil the leaf in water

4) Soak the leaf in warm alcohol to make it go colourless

6) Drip brown iodine solution onto the leaf

3) If the _iodine_ goes _dark blue/black_ then _starch is present_, showing _that bit of leaf_ was managing to do _photosynthesis_.

4) If the iodine _stays brown_ then there's _no starch_, which shows that part of the leaf was **NOT** managing to do photosynthesis — because it _wasn't getting_ either _light_ or CO_2.

2) Testing Water uptake With a Potometer

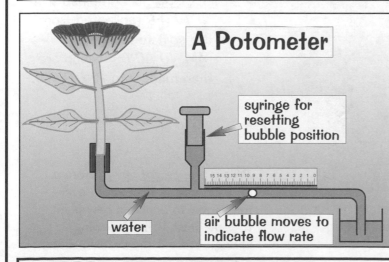

A Potometer

syringe for resetting bubble position

water

air bubble moves to indicate flow rate

1) This experiment allows you to test the _rate of water uptake_ of a plant in various _atmospheric conditions_.

2) As water _evaporates_ from the leaves, it _draws it up_ the stem and the _bubble_ moves along the tube.

3) The _further_ the bubble travels in a given time, the _faster_ the rate of _water uptake_ or _transpiration_.

4) You can expose the plant to _wind_ or _heat_ or _moisture_ etc., to see how it affects the rate of water uptake.

Test Yourself Here to find out what you've taken in...

Two simple experiments that you should be familiar with. In the Exam they may give you a question based on either of these. You need to know the _significance_ of what happens in each experiment. _Learn the diagrams and the words_. Practise with the _scribbled 'mini-essay' method_.

How Plants Use The Glucose

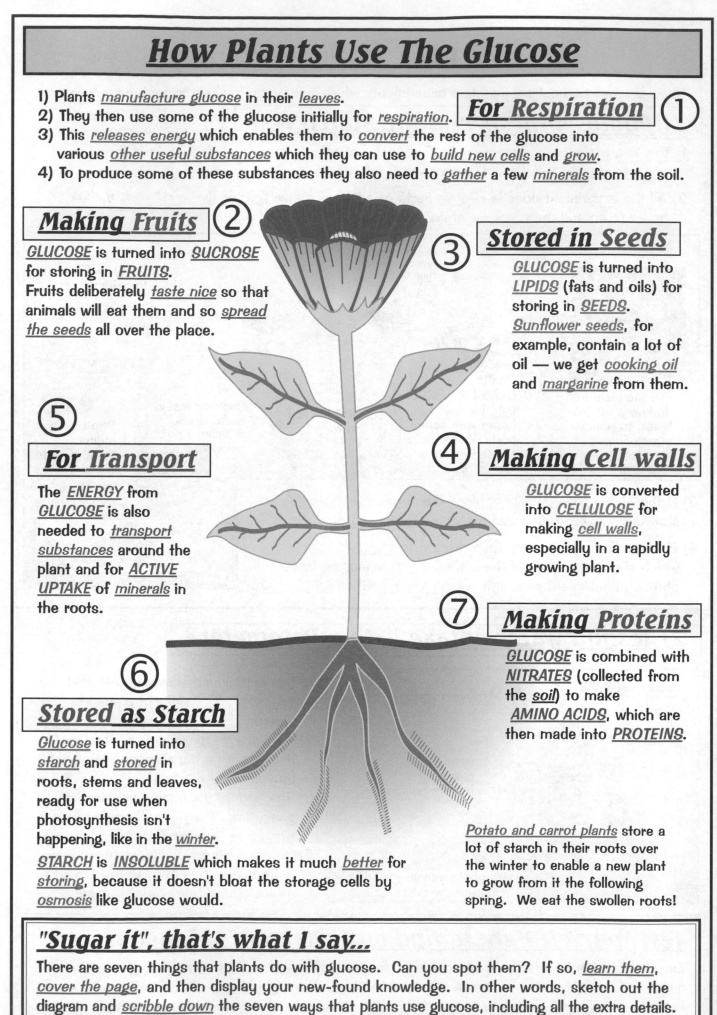

1) Plants _manufacture glucose_ in their _leaves_.
2) They then use some of the glucose initially for _respiration_.
3) This _releases energy_ which enables them to _convert_ the rest of the glucose into various _other useful substances_ which they can use to _build new cells_ and _grow_.
4) To produce some of these substances they also need to _gather_ a few _minerals_ from the soil.

For Respiration ①

Making Fruits ②

GLUCOSE is turned into _SUCROSE_ for storing in _FRUITS_.
Fruits deliberately _taste nice_ so that animals will eat them and so _spread the seeds_ all over the place.

③ Stored in Seeds

GLUCOSE is turned into _LIPIDS_ (fats and oils) for storing in _SEEDS_.
Sunflower seeds, for example, contain a lot of oil — we get _cooking oil_ and _margarine_ from them.

⑤ For Transport

The _ENERGY_ from _GLUCOSE_ is also needed to _transport substances_ around the plant and for _ACTIVE UPTAKE_ of _minerals_ in the roots.

④ Making Cell walls

GLUCOSE is converted into _CELLULOSE_ for making _cell walls_, especially in a rapidly growing plant.

⑦ Making Proteins

GLUCOSE is combined with _NITRATES_ (collected from the _soil_) to make _AMINO ACIDS_, which are then made into _PROTEINS_.

⑥ Stored as Starch

Glucose is turned into _starch_ and _stored_ in roots, stems and leaves, ready for use when photosynthesis isn't happening, like in the _winter_.
STARCH is _INSOLUBLE_ which makes it much _better_ for _storing_, because it doesn't bloat the storage cells by _osmosis_ like glucose would.

Potato and carrot plants store a lot of starch in their roots over the winter to enable a new plant to grow from it the following spring. We eat the swollen roots!

"Sugar it", that's what I say...

There are seven things that plants do with glucose. Can you spot them? If so, _learn them_, _cover the page_, and then display your new-found knowledge. In other words, sketch out the diagram and _scribble down_ the seven ways that plants use glucose, including all the extra details.

Minerals Needed For Healthy Growth

For _healthy growth_ plants need these three really important minerals which they can only obtain _from the soil_ through their _roots_:

The Three Essential Minerals

1) Nitrates

— for making _AMINO ACIDS_ and for the "synthesis" (making) of _PROTEINS_ and _DNA_.

2) Phosphates

— have an important role in reactions involved in _PHOTOSYNTHESIS_ and _RESPIRATION_. The element _PHOSPHORUS_ is also used to make _DNA_ and _CELL MEMBRANES_.

3) Potassium

— helps the _ENZYMES_ involved in _PHOTOSYNTHESIS_ and _RESPIRATION_ to work.

Iron and Magnesium are also needed in Small Amounts

The three main minerals are needed in fairly large amounts, but there are other elements which are needed in much smaller amounts. _IRON_ and _MAGNESIUM_ are the most significant as they're required for making _CHLOROPHYLL_, which is pretty important to plants, in case you didn't know.

Lack of These Nutrients Causes Deficiency Symptoms:

1) Lack of Nitrates

— _STUNTED GROWTH_ and _YELLOW OLDER LEAVES_.

2) Lack of Phosphates

— _POOR ROOT GROWTH_ and _PURPLE YOUNGER LEAVES_.

3) Lack of Potassium

— _YELLOW LEAVES_ with _DEAD SPOTS_.

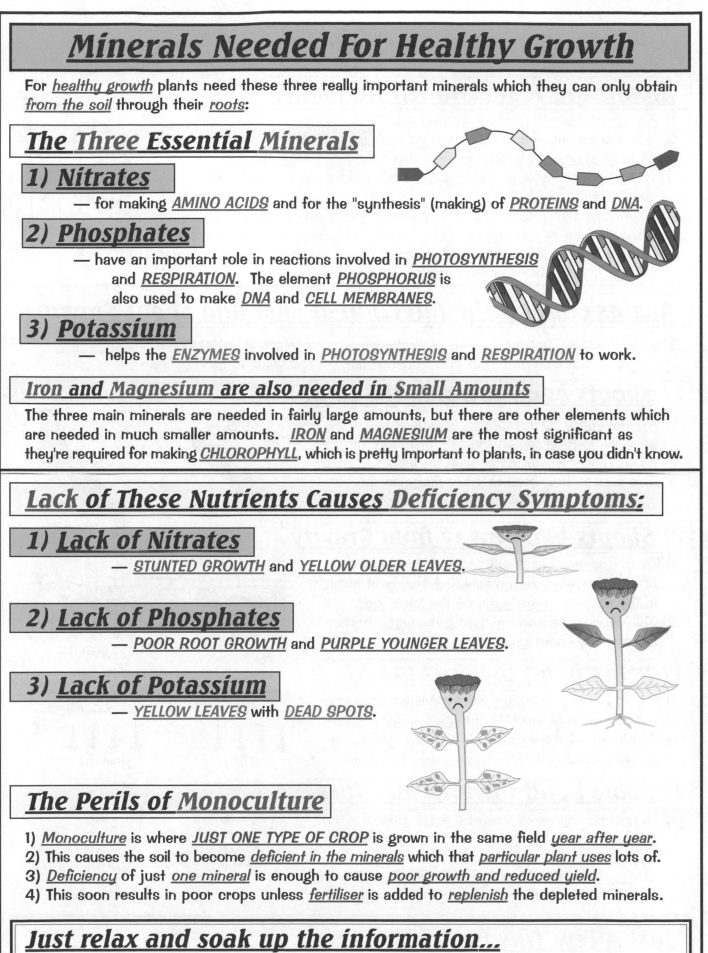

The Perils of Monoculture

1) _Monoculture_ is where _JUST ONE TYPE OF CROP_ is grown in the same field _year after year_.
2) This causes the soil to become _deficient in the minerals_ which that _particular plant uses_ lots of.
3) _Deficiency_ of just _one mineral_ is enough to cause _poor growth and reduced yield_.
4) This soon results in poor crops unless _fertiliser_ is added to _replenish_ the depleted minerals.

Just relax and soak up the information...

Very straightforward learning here. Two nice big clear sections with all the important bits highlighted in colour as usual. You should be able to _cover this page_ and _scribble_ virtually the whole thing down again with very little bother. _Learn and enjoy._

Growth Hormones in Plants

Auxins are Plant Growth Hormones

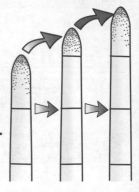

1) _Auxins_ are _hormones_ which _control growth_ at the _tips_ of _shoots_ and _roots_.
2) Auxin is produced in the _tips_ and _diffuses backwards_ to stimulate the _cell elongation process_ which occurs in the cells _just behind_ the tips.
3) If the tip of a shoot is _removed_, no auxin will be available and the shoot _may stop growing_.
4) Shoot tips also produce substances which _inhibit_ the growth of _side shoots_. If the tips are _removed_ it can result in a lot of _side shoots_ because the inhibitor substance is no longer present. Hence, _hedge clipping_ promotes _bushier hedges_, because it produces lots of side shoots.

Auxins Change The Direction of Root and Shoot Growth

You'll note below that extra auxin _promotes growth in the shoot_ but actually _inhibits growth in the root_, — but also note that this produces the _desired result_ in _both cases_.

1) Shoots bend towards the light

1) When a _shoot tip_ is _exposed to light_, it provides _more auxin_ on the side that is in the _shade_ than the side which is in the light.
2) This causes the shoot to grow _faster_ on the _shaded side_ and it bends _towards_ the light.

2) Shoots bend away from Gravity

1) When a _shoot_ finds itself growing _sideways_, the gravity produces an unequal distribution of auxin in the tip, with _more auxin_ on the _lower side_.
2) This causes the lower side to grow _faster_, thus bending the shoot _upwards_.

gravity   gravity

3) Roots bend towards Gravity

1) A _root_ growing _sideways_ will experience the same redistribution of auxin to the _lower side_.
2) But in a root the _extra auxin_ actually _inhibits_ growth, causing it to bend _downwards_ instead.

gravity   gravity

4) Roots bend towards Moisture

1) An uneven degree of moisture either side of a root will cause _more auxin_ to appear on the side with _more moisture_.
2) This _inhibits_ growth on that side, causing the root to grow in that direction, _towards the moisture_.

moisture   moisture

Just A Few Tips for Your Revision...

An easy page to learn. Just four points on auxins, together with a diagram, and then four ways that shoots and roots change direction, with a diagram for each. You just have to _learn it_. Then _cover the page_ and _scribble down_ the main points _from memory_. Then try again, and again...

Commercial Use of Plant Hormones

Plant hormones have a lot of uses in the _food growing business_.

1) Producing Seedless Fruit

1) Fruits normally only grow on plants which have been _pollinated by insects_, with the inevitable _seeds_ in the middle of the fruit. If the plant _doesn't_ get pollinated, the fruits and seeds _don't grow_.
2) However, if _growth hormones_ are applied to _unpollinated flowers_ the _fruits will grow_ but the _seeds won't_!
3) This is great. Seedless satsumas and seedless grapes are just _so much nicer_ than the 'natural' ones full of pips!

Hmmph!

(Redundant bee)

Unpollinated flower

Wonderful seedless grapes

2) Controlling the Ripening of Fruit

1) The _ripening_ of fruits can be controlled either while they are _still on the plant_, or during _transport_ to the shops.
2) This allows the fruit to be picked while it's still _unripe_ (and therefore firmer and _less easily damaged_).
3) It can then be sprayed with _ripening hormone_ and it will ripen _on the way to the supermarket_ to be perfect just as it reaches the shelves.

3) Growing from Cuttings with Rooting Compound

1) A _cutting_ is part of a plant that has been _cut off it_, like the end of a branch with a few leaves on it.
2) Normally, if you stick cuttings in the soil they _won't grow_, but if you add _rooting compound_, which is a plant _growth hormone_, they will produce roots rapidly and start growing as _new plants_.
3) This enables growers to produce lots of _clones_ (exact copies) of a really good plant _very quickly_.

boring old soil

rooting compound

4) Killing Weeds

1) Most weeds growing in fields of crops or in a lawn are _broad-leaved_, in contrast to grass which has very _narrow leaves_.
2) _Selective weedkillers_ have been developed from _plant growth hormones_ which only affect the broad-leaved plants.
3) They totally _disrupt_ their normal _growth patterns_, which soon _kills_ them, whilst leaving the grass untouched.

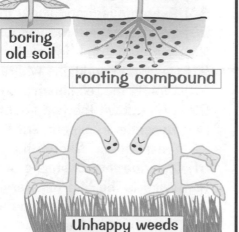

Unhappy weeds

Remember, serious learning always bears fruit...

Another blissfully easy page. Just make sure you learn enough about each bit to answer a 3 mark Exam question on it (that means being able to make 3 valid points). As usual the sections are split into numbered points to help you remember them. They've all got three points to learn. _So learn them_. Then _cover the page_ and _scribble down_ the 3 points for each . And tell me this: — if you can't do it now, what makes you think it'll all suddenly _"come back to you"_ in the Exam?

Revision Summary For Section One

There's a lot of real easy stuff on plants, that's for sure. But easy stuff means easy marks, and you better make sure you get all the easy marks — every last one. There's nothing quite as spectacularly dumb as working really hard at the difficult stuff and then forgetting about the easy bits. Here's some tough questions on plants for you. Practise them over and over and over until you can just glide through them all, like a swan or something.

1) What use is Mrs Nerg?
2) Sketch an animal cell and a plant cell with the seven labels.
3) Sketch five different plant cells and explain how they're specialised for their job.
4) Give an example of this sequence: cells → tissues → organ → organism.
5) Give the strict definition of diffusion. Sketch how a smell diffuses through air in a room.
6) Which three gases diffuse in and out of leaves? What process are they involved with?
7) Why are cell membranes kinda clever? What will and won't diffuse through cell membranes?
8) What happens at root hairs? What process is involved? Which process *won't* work there?
9) Give the full strict definition of osmosis. What does it do to plant and animal cells in water?
10) What is visking tubing? What will and won't pass through it?
11) Give full details of the potato tubes experiment and the visking tubing experiment.
12) Sketch a typical plant and label the five important parts. Explain exactly what each bit does.
13) Sketch the cross-section of a leaf with seven labels. What is the leaf for?
14) Give five written details about the leaf structure in relation to what the leaf needs to do.
15) Explain what stomata do and how they do it.
16) What is transpiration? What causes it? What benefits does it bring?
17) What are the four factors which affect the rate of transpiration?
18) What is turgor pressure? How does is come about and what use is it to plants?
19) What are the two types of tubes in plants? Whereabouts are they found in plants?
20) List three features for both types of tube and sketch them both.
21) Sketch a root and say what goes on in the tubes inside it.
22) What does photosynthesis do? Where does it do it?
23) Write down the word and symbol equations for photosynthesis.
24) Sketch a leaf and show the four things needed for photosynthesis.
25) What are the three variable quantities which affect the rate of photosynthesis?
26) Sketch a graph for each one and explain the shape.
27) Describe conditions where each of the three factors is in short supply.
28) What's the relationship between photosynthesis and respiration?
29) Write down the two equations, and say which way the energy goes in each one.
30) Describe an experiment to demonstrate the interplay between photosynthesis and respiration. Sketch the graphs and explain their shape. What is the effect of animals?
31) Describe the six stages of an experiment to demonstrate when photosynthesis will happen.
32) What is the test for starch?
33) Sketch a potometer and explain what it can demonstrate and measure.
34) Sketch a plant and label the seven ways that plants use glucose.
35) Give a couple of extra details for each of the seven uses.
36) List the five main minerals needed for healthy plant growth, and what they're needed for.
37) What are the three deficiency symptoms? What are the perils of monoculture?
38) What are auxins? Where are they produced? What happens if you cut a shoot tip off?
39) There are four ways that auxins affect roots and shoots. Give full details for all four.
40) List the four commercial uses for plant hormones. How are seedless grapes made?
41) Explain what rooting compound is used for. How do hormonal weed killers work?

Nutrition

There are _seven_ different types of _"nutrients"_ which all animals need in their diet.
Make sure you know all about them:

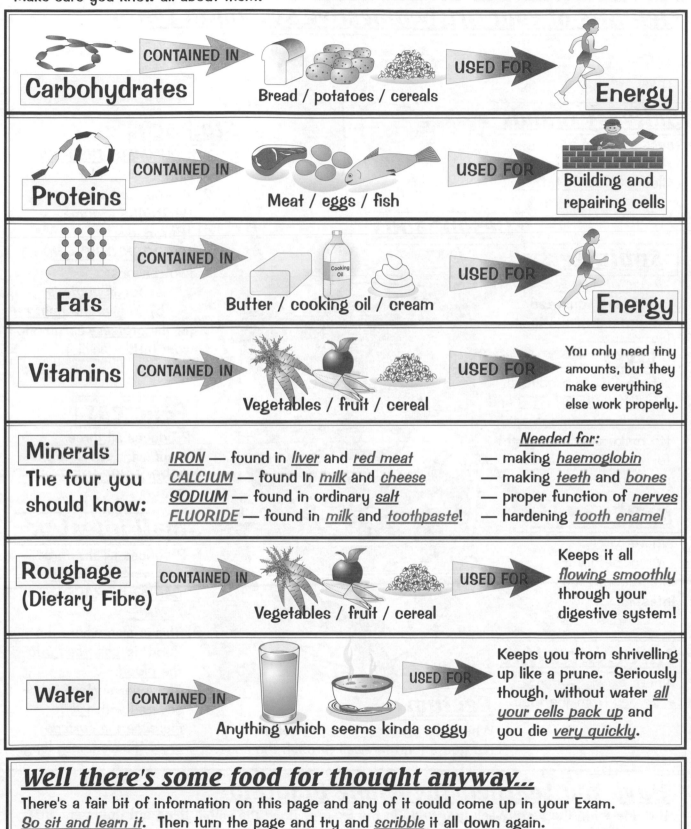

Carbohydrates CONTAINED IN Bread / potatoes / cereals USED FOR **Energy**

Proteins CONTAINED IN Meat / eggs / fish USED FOR Building and repairing cells

Fats CONTAINED IN Butter / cooking oil / cream USED FOR **Energy**

Vitamins CONTAINED IN Vegetables / fruit / cereal USED FOR You only need tiny amounts, but they make everything else work properly.

Minerals
The four you should know:

IRON — found in _liver_ and _red meat_
CALCIUM — found In _milk_ and _cheese_
SODIUM — found in ordinary _salt_
FLUORIDE — found in _milk_ and _toothpaste_!

Needed for:
— making _haemoglobin_
— making _teeth_ and _bones_
— proper function of _nerves_
— hardening _tooth enamel_

Roughage
(Dietary Fibre) CONTAINED IN Vegetables / fruit / cereal USED FOR Keeps it all _flowing smoothly_ through your digestive system!

Water CONTAINED IN Anything which seems kinda soggy USED FOR Keeps you from shrivelling up like a prune. Seriously though, without water _all your cells pack up_ and you die _very quickly_.

Well there's some food for thought anyway...

There's a fair bit of information on this page and any of it could come up in your Exam.
So sit and learn it. Then turn the page and try and _scribble_ it all down again.
And just keep practising till you can answer these two questions without looking back.

1) What are the seven different types of nutrient? What is each one used for in your body?
2) _For each one_ name _three_ foods which contain them.

The Digestive System

You'll definitely get a question on this in your Exam so take your time and learn this very important diagram in all its infinite glory. And that includes the words too:

Ten Bits of Your Grisly Digestive System to Learn:

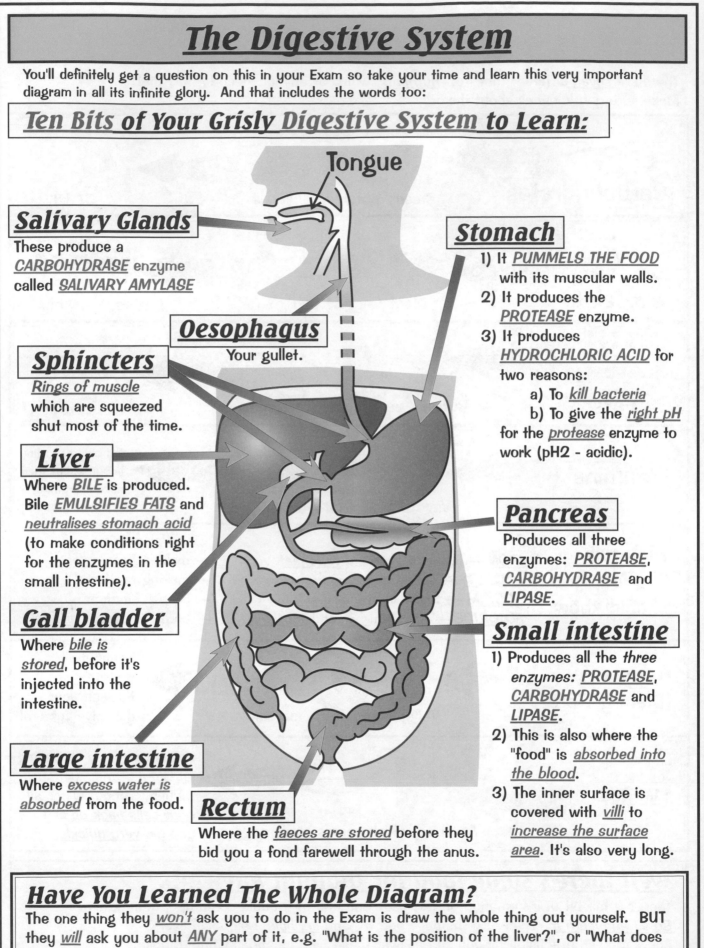

Tongue

Salivary Glands
These produce a _CARBOHYDRASE_ enzyme called _SALIVARY AMYLASE_

Oesophagus
Your gullet.

Sphincters
Rings of muscle which are squeezed shut most of the time.

Liver
Where _BILE_ is produced. Bile _EMULSIFIES FATS_ and _neutralises stomach acid_ (to make conditions right for the enzymes in the small intestine).

Gall bladder
Where _bile is stored_, before it's injected into the intestine.

Large intestine
Where _excess water is absorbed_ from the food.

Stomach
1) It _PUMMELS THE FOOD_ with its muscular walls.
2) It produces the _PROTEASE_ enzyme.
3) It produces _HYDROCHLORIC ACID_ for two reasons:
    a) To _kill bacteria_
    b) To give the _right pH_ for the _protease_ enzyme to work (pH2 - acidic).

Pancreas
Produces all three enzymes: _PROTEASE_, _CARBOHYDRASE_ and _LIPASE_.

Small intestine
1) Produces all the _three_ enzymes: _PROTEASE_, _CARBOHYDRASE_ and _LIPASE_.
2) This is also where the "food" is _absorbed into the blood_.
3) The inner surface is covered with _villi_ to _increase the surface area_. It's also very long.

Rectum
Where the _faeces are stored_ before they bid you a fond farewell through the anus.

Have You Learned The Whole Diagram?
The one thing they _won't_ ask you to do in the Exam is draw the whole thing out yourself. BUT they _will_ ask you about _ANY_ part of it, e.g. "What is the position of the liver?", or "What does the pancreas produce?", or "What is the function of bile?" So in the end you have to _learn_ the whole thing anyway. And that means being able to _cover the page_ and draw it out, _words and all_. If you can't draw it all out _from memory_ — then you haven't learnt it. Simple as that.

Digestive Enzymes

There are only _THREE MAIN DIGESTIVE ENZYMES_. Sadly they all have silly names that can be hard to learn and their "products of digestion" all have suitably silly names too. Ah well — that's Biology for you!

Enzymes break down Big Molecules into Small Ones

1) _Starch_, _proteins_ and _fats_ are _big molecules_ which can't pass through cell walls into the blood.
2) _Sugars_, _amino acids_ and _fatty acids/glycerol_ are _much smaller molecules_ which can pass easily into the blood.
3) _Enzymes_ act as _catalysts_ to break down the _big molecules_ into the _smaller ones_.

1) Carbohydrase Converts Starch into Simple Sugars

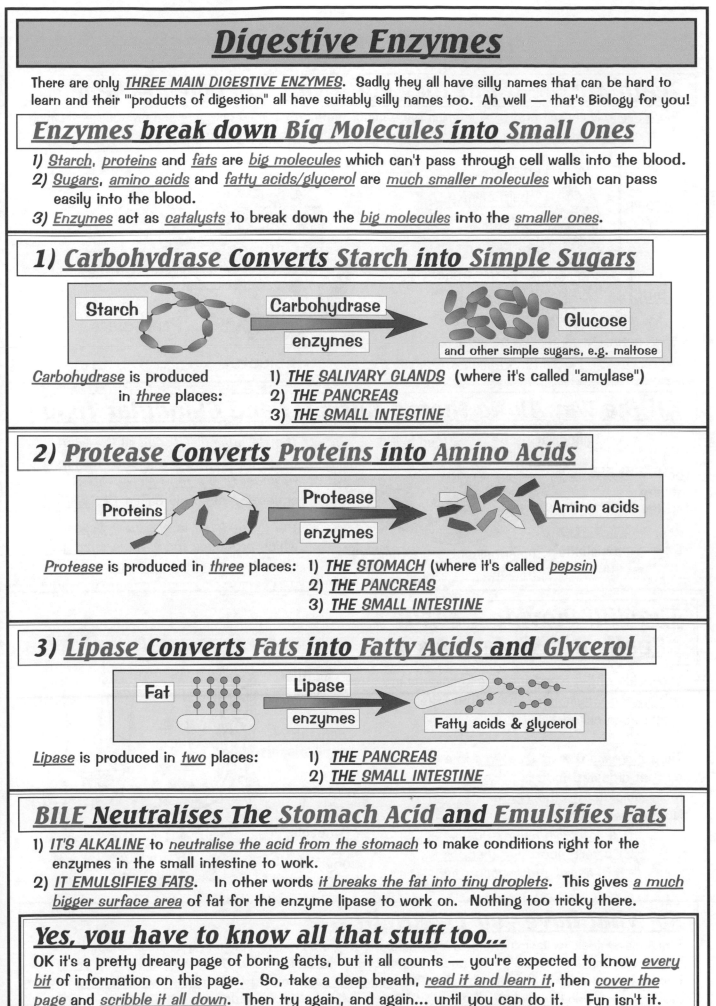

Starch → Carbohydrase enzymes → Glucose
and other simple sugars, e.g. maltose

Carbohydrase is produced in _three_ places:
1) _THE SALIVARY GLANDS_ (where it's called "amylase")
2) _THE PANCREAS_
3) _THE SMALL INTESTINE_

2) Protease Converts Proteins into Amino Acids

Proteins → Protease enzymes → Amino acids

Protease is produced in _three_ places:
1) _THE STOMACH_ (where it's called _pepsin_)
2) _THE PANCREAS_
3) _THE SMALL INTESTINE_

3) Lipase Converts Fats into Fatty Acids and Glycerol

Fat → Lipase enzymes → Fatty acids & glycerol

Lipase is produced in _two_ places:
1) _THE PANCREAS_
2) _THE SMALL INTESTINE_

BILE Neutralises The Stomach Acid and Emulsifies Fats

1) _IT'S ALKALINE_ to _neutralise the acid from the stomach_ to make conditions right for the enzymes in the small intestine to work.
2) _IT EMULSIFIES FATS_.   In other words _it breaks the fat into tiny droplets_. This gives _a much bigger surface area_ of fat for the enzyme lipase to work on. Nothing too tricky there.

Yes, you have to know all that stuff too...

OK it's a pretty dreary page of boring facts, but it all counts — you're expected to know _every bit_ of information on this page. So, take a deep breath, _read it and learn it_, then _cover the page_ and _scribble it all down_. Then try again, and again... until you can do it.   Fun isn't it.

Digestive System Extras

Teeth are Great but they Rot if you don't Clean Them

Tooth decay is caused by _bacteria_ which live on your teeth. They feed on _sugar_ and produce _acid_ which _dissolves_ your teeth. _Fluoride_ in _toothpaste_ helps _strengthen the enamel_ to resist acid attack.

Make sure you know the _four different types_ of teeth:

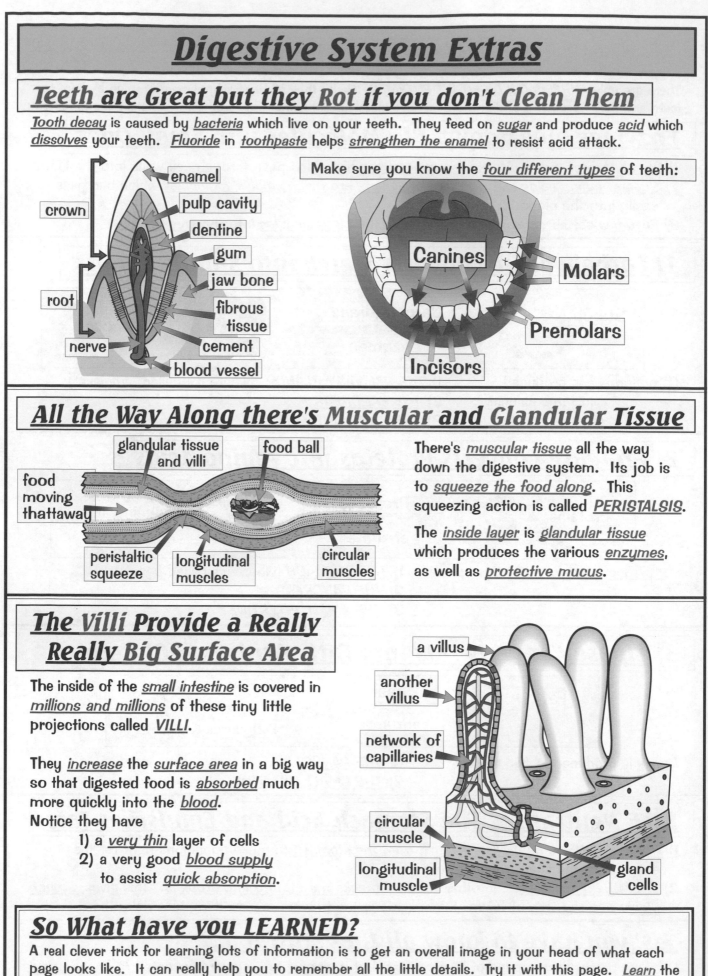

Diagram labels: crown, enamel, pulp cavity, dentine, gum, jaw bone, root, fibrous tissue, nerve, cement, blood vessel

Teeth types: Canines, Molars, Premolars, Incisors

All the Way Along there's Muscular and Glandular Tissue

Diagram labels: glandular tissue and villi, food ball, food moving thattaway, peristaltic squeeze, longitudinal muscles, circular muscles

There's _muscular tissue_ all the way down the digestive system. Its job is to _squeeze the food along_. This squeezing action is called _PERISTALSIS_.

The _inside layer_ is _glandular tissue_ which produces the various _enzymes_, as well as _protective mucus_.

The Villi Provide a Really Really Big Surface Area

The inside of the _small intestine_ is covered in _millions and millions_ of these tiny little projections called _VILLI_.

They _increase_ the _surface area_ in a big way so that digested food is _absorbed_ much more quickly into the _blood_.
Notice they have
1) a _very thin_ layer of cells
2) a very good _blood supply_
    to assist _quick absorption_.

Diagram labels: a villus, another villus, network of capillaries, circular muscle, longitudinal muscle, gland cells

So What have you LEARNED?

A real clever trick for learning lots of information is to get an overall image in your head of what each page looks like. It can really help you to remember all the little details. Try it with this page. _Learn_ the four diagrams, with all their little labels. Then _cover the page_ and try and _picture the whole thing_ in your head. Then try and _scribble it all down_. It takes practise but you _can_ do it.

Diffusion of "Food" Molecules

The Big Food Molecules Must First be Broken Down

After you've _chewed_ your food up and then your _stomach's had its turn_ at munching it up still further, it's still made up of _quite big molecules_, namely: _STARCH_, _PROTEINS_ and _FATS_. These are still _TOO BIG_ to diffuse into the blood, and so they are _broken down_ in the _small intestine_ into _smaller molecules_: _GLUCOSE_, _AMINO ACIDS_ and _FATTY ACIDS_ & _GLYCEROL_.

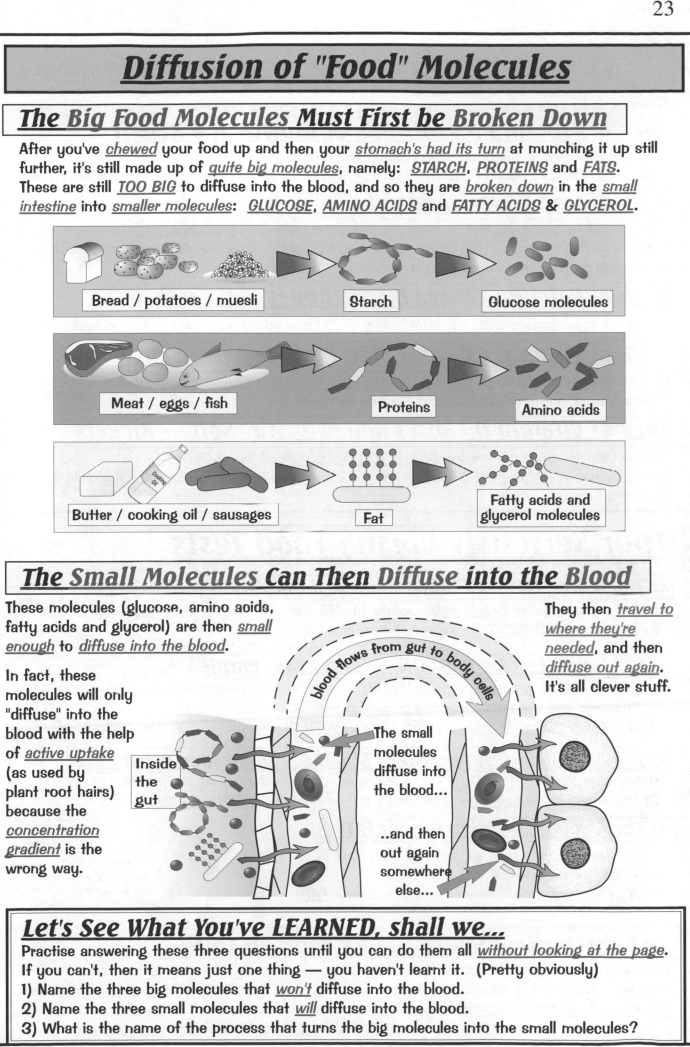

Bread / potatoes / muesli → Starch → Glucose molecules

Meat / eggs / fish → Proteins → Amino acids

Butter / cooking oil / sausages → Fat → Fatty acids and glycerol molecules

The Small Molecules Can Then Diffuse into the Blood

These molecules (glucose, amino acids, fatty acids and glycerol) are then _small enough_ to _diffuse into the blood_.

In fact, these molecules will only "diffuse" into the blood with the help of _active uptake_ (as used by plant root hairs) because the _concentration gradient_ is the wrong way.

Inside the gut

blood flows from gut to body cells

The small molecules diffuse into the blood...

..and then out again somewhere else...

They then _travel to where they're needed_, and then _diffuse out again_. It's all clever stuff.

Let's See What You've LEARNED, shall we...

Practise answering these three questions until you can do them all _without looking at the page_. If you can't, then it means just one thing — you haven't learnt it. (Pretty obviously)
1) Name the three big molecules that _won't_ diffuse into the blood.
2) Name the three small molecules that _will_ diffuse into the blood.
3) What is the name of the process that turns the big molecules into the small molecules?

Nutrient Deficiencies and Food Tests

This is a really boring page.

Lack of Protein Prevents proper Growth and Repair

As well as preventing the body from growing and repairing itself properly, lack of protein also causes a disease called KWASHIORKOR which causes the stomach to become bloated.

Lack of Iron Causes Anaemia

Lack of Iron causes ANAEMIA because the red blood cells don't contain enough haemoglobin, which is made from iron. This makes the person look pale. They also feel tired because their blood can't carry enough oxygen to their cells.

Lack of Calcium Causes Brittle Bones and Teeth

Lack of Calcium causes BRITTLE BONES AND TEETH and poor growth of bones and teeth in kids.

Lack of Vitamin C Causes Skin Problems like Scurvy

Lack of vitamin C causes SCURVY AND OTHER SKIN DISORDERS. Without vitamin C the skin becomes weak and cracks open, and wounds do not heal.

Lack of Vitamin D Causes Bones to Stay Soft — Rickets

Not enough vitamin D causes the BONES TO STAY SOFT and they bend.
This is known as RICKETS and it usually shows up as "bow legs" which happens if a child grows up without enough vitamin D.

Four Seriously boring Food Tests

1) The Iodine Test for STARCH — turns it Blue/black

1) Add some drops of brown iodine solution to the food.
2) If it contains STARCH the iodine will turn blue/black.

Starch for sure

2) The Biuret test for PROTEIN — turns CuSO₄ Purple

1) First add some sodium hydroxide (NaOH) solution and shake with care.
2) Then add some weak copper sulphate solution.
3) If the pale blue colour turns purple there's PROTEIN present.

Protein for sure

3) The Benedict's test for SIMPLE SUGARS — an Orange Precipitate

1) Add blue BENEDICT'S SOLUTION to the food in a test tube. Bring to the boil.
2) If you get an orange precipitate then the food contains SIMPLE SUGARS.

4) The Alcohol-Emulsion test for FATS

1) Mix the food with pure ethanol and then filter it.
2) Add the clear solution to water.
3) A white emulsion indicates the food contains FATS.

Milky emulsion – Fat for sure

Got any Deficiencies? — Test Yourself Here...

What a grim-looking page this is. No decent diagrams, just lots of boring facts.
Trouble is you've still gotta learn it. Toughsky. You know the drill though: cover the page, then scribble it down from memory until you remember all the facts without having to look back.
Remember, this book isn't full of drivel. Just all the basic facts which YOU have to learn.

The Circulatory System

The circulatory system's main function is to get food and oxygen to every cell in the body. The diagram shows the basic layout, but make sure you learn the five important points too.

The DOUBLE Circulatory System, actually

① The **HEART** is actually **TWO PUMPS**. The **RIGHT SIDE** pumps deoxygenated blood to the **LUNGS** to **COLLECT OXYGEN**. Then the **LEFT SIDE** pumps this oxygenated blood **AROUND THE BODY**.

② **ARTERIES** carry blood *away from the heart* at **HIGH PRESSURE**.

③ Normally, arteries carry **OXYGENATED BLOOD** and veins carry **DEOXYGENATED BLOOD**.

The *pulmonary artery* and *pulmonary vein* are the *big exceptions* to this rule (see diagram).

④ The arteries eventually **SPLIT OFF** into *thousands of tiny capillaries* which take blood to *every cell in the body*.

⑤ The **VEINS** then collect the *"used" blood* and carry it *back to the heart* at *low pressure* to be pumped round again.

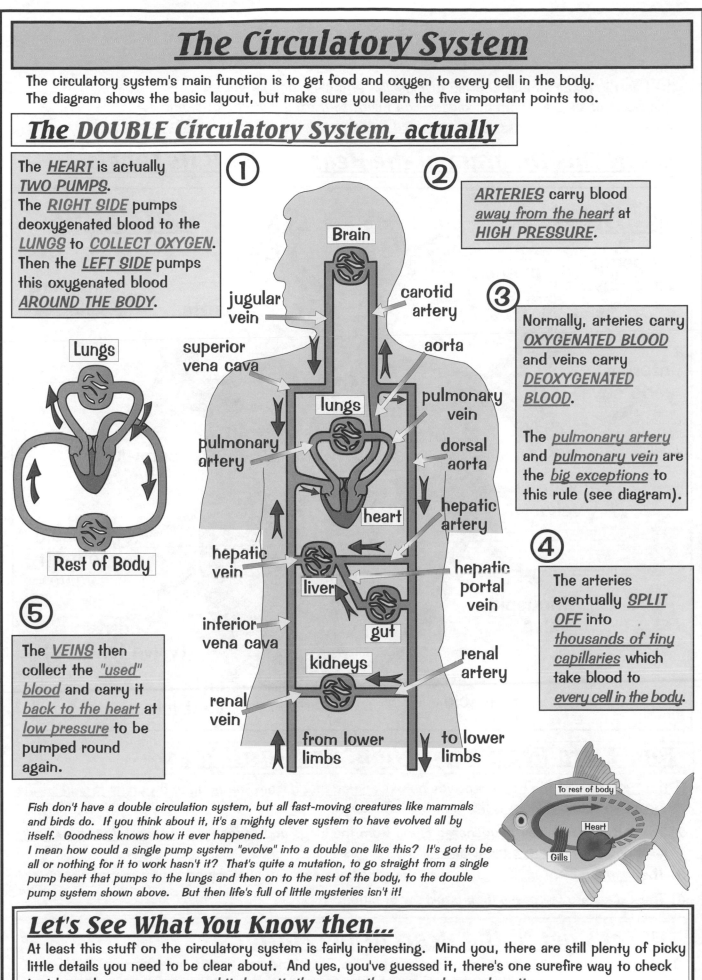

Lungs
Rest of Body

Brain
jugular vein
carotid artery
superior vena cava
aorta
lungs
pulmonary vein
pulmonary artery
dorsal aorta
heart
hepatic artery
hepatic vein
liver
hepatic portal vein
inferior vena cava
gut
kidneys
renal artery
renal vein
from lower limbs
to lower limbs

To rest of body
Heart
Gills

Fish don't have a double circulation system, but all fast-moving creatures like mammals and birds do. If you think about it, it's a mighty clever system to have evolved all by itself. Goodness knows how it ever happened.
I mean how could a single pump system "evolve" into a double one like this? It's got to be all or nothing for it to work hasn't it? That's quite a mutation, to go straight from a single pump heart that pumps to the lungs and then on to the rest of the body, to the double pump system shown above. But then life's full of little mysteries isn't it!

Let's See What You Know then...

At least this stuff on the circulatory system is fairly interesting. Mind you, there are still plenty of picky little details you need to be clear about. And yes, you've guessed it, there's one surefire way to check just how clear you are — *read it, learn it, then cover the page and reproduce it*.
Having to sketch the diagram out again *from memory* is the only way to *really learn it*.

The Heart

The heart is made almost entirely of _muscle_. And it's a _double pump_.
Visualise this diagram with its _bigger side_ full of _red, oxygenated blood_, and
its _smaller side_ full of _blue, deoxygenated blood_, and learn that the _left side_ is _bigger_.

Learn This Diagram of the Heart with All its Labels

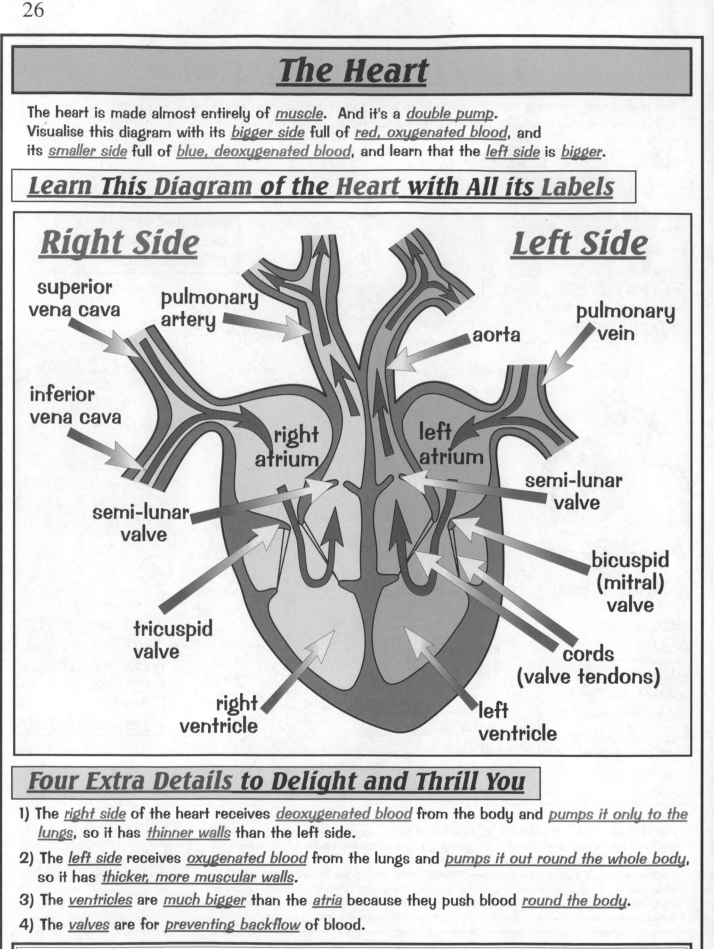

Four Extra Details to Delight and Thrill You

1) The _right side_ of the heart receives _deoxygenated blood_ from the body and _pumps it only to the lungs_, so it has _thinner walls_ than the left side.

2) The _left side_ receives _oxygenated blood_ from the lungs and _pumps it out round the whole body_, so it has _thicker, more muscular walls_.

3) The _ventricles_ are _much bigger_ than the _atria_ because they push blood _round the body_.

4) The _valves_ are for _preventing backflow_ of blood.

OK Let's get to the Heart of the Matter...

They quite often put a diagram of the heart in the Exam and ask you to label parts of it.
There's only one way to be sure you can label it all and that's to learn the diagram until you can
sketch it out, with all the labels, _from memory_. Also _learn_ the four points at the bottom.

The Pumping Cycle

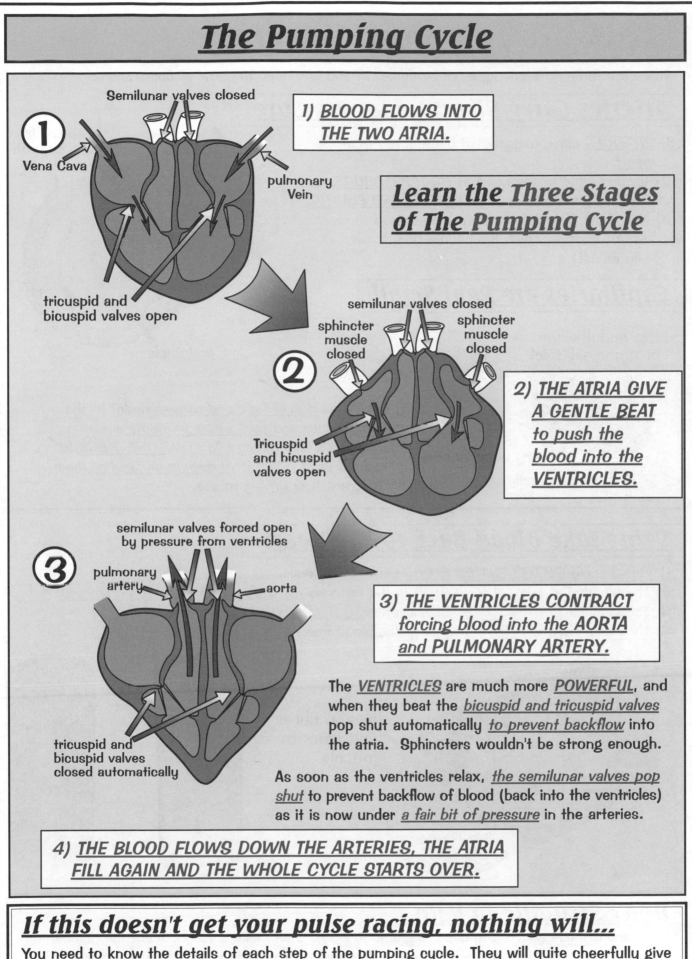

1) BLOOD FLOWS INTO THE TWO ATRIA.

Semilunar valves closed

Vena Cava

pulmonary Vein

tricuspid and bicuspid valves open

Learn the Three Stages of The Pumping Cycle

semilunar valves closed

sphincter muscle closed

sphincter muscle closed

Tricuspid and bicuspid valves open

2) THE ATRIA GIVE A GENTLE BEAT _to push the_ blood into the VENTRICLES.

semilunar valves forced open by pressure from ventricles

pulmonary artery

aorta

tricuspid and bicuspid valves closed automatically

3) THE VENTRICLES CONTRACT _forcing blood into the AORTA and PULMONARY ARTERY._

The _VENTRICLES_ are much more _POWERFUL_, and when they beat the _bicuspid and tricuspid valves_ pop shut automatically _to prevent backflow_ into the atria. Sphincters wouldn't be strong enough.

As soon as the ventricles relax, _the semilunar valves pop shut_ to prevent backflow of blood (back into the ventricles) as it is now under _a fair bit of pressure_ in the arteries.

4) THE BLOOD FLOWS DOWN THE ARTERIES, THE ATRIA FILL AGAIN AND THE WHOLE CYCLE STARTS OVER.

If this doesn't get your pulse racing, nothing will...

You need to know the details of each step of the pumping cycle. They will quite cheerfully give you a diagram similar to one of the above and ask you which valves are open or where the blood is flowing etc. etc. Make sure you can _sketch out_ all three diagrams _from memory_.

Blood Vessels

There are three different types of blood vessel and you need to know all about them:

Arteries Carry Blood Under Pressure

1) _ARTERIES_ carry oxygenated blood _away from the heart_.
2) It comes out of the heart at _HIGH PRESSURE_, so the artery walls have to be _STRONG AND ELASTIC_.
3) Note how _THICK_ the walls are compared to the size of the hole down the middle (the "lumen" — silly name!)

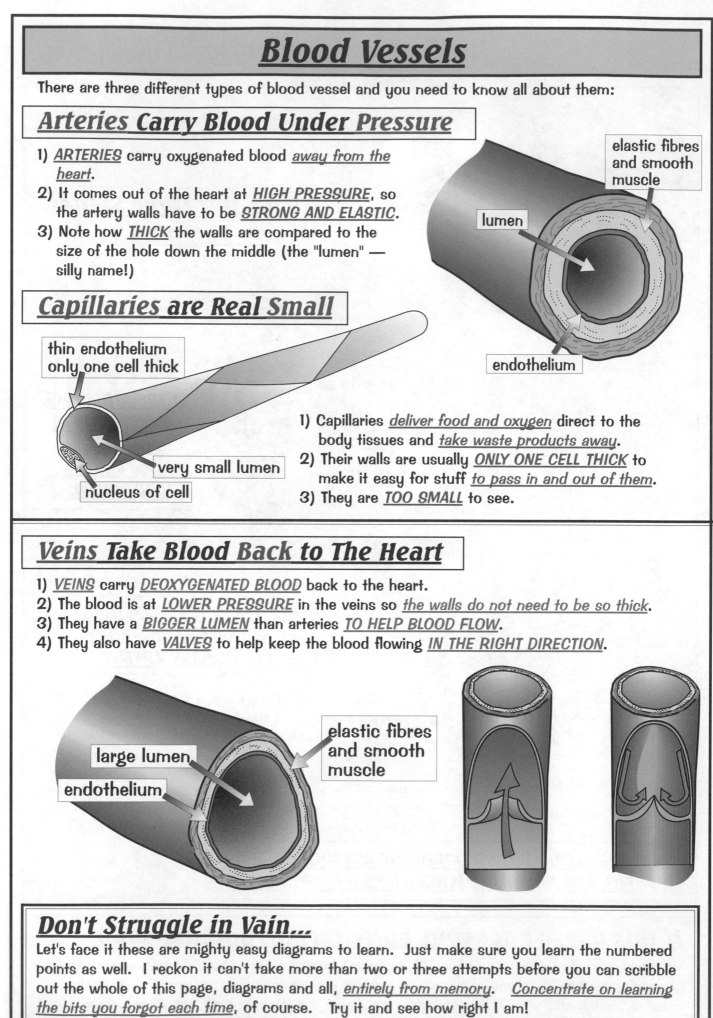

elastic fibres and smooth muscle

lumen

endothelium

Capillaries are Real Small

thin endothelium only one cell thick

very small lumen

nucleus of cell

1) Capillaries _deliver food and oxygen_ direct to the body tissues and _take waste products away_.
2) Their walls are usually _ONLY ONE CELL THICK_ to make it easy for stuff _to pass in and out of them_.
3) They are _TOO SMALL_ to see.

Veins Take Blood Back to The Heart

1) _VEINS_ carry _DEOXYGENATED BLOOD_ back to the heart.
2) The blood is at _LOWER PRESSURE_ in the veins so _the walls do not need to be so thick_.
3) They have a _BIGGER LUMEN_ than arteries _TO HELP BLOOD FLOW_.
4) They also have _VALVES_ to help keep the blood flowing _IN THE RIGHT DIRECTION_.

large lumen

endothelium

elastic fibres and smooth muscle

Don't Struggle in Vain...

Let's face it these are mighty easy diagrams to learn. Just make sure you learn the numbered points as well. I reckon it can't take more than two or three attempts before you can scribble out the whole of this page, diagrams and all, _entirely from memory_. _Concentrate on learning the bits you forgot each time_, of course. Try it and see how right I am!

Blood

Red Blood Cells

1) Their job is to *CARRY OXYGEN* to all the cells in the body.
2) They have a *FLYING DOUGHNUT SHAPE* to give *MAXIMUM SURFACE AREA* for *absorbing oxygen*.
3) They contain *HAEMOGLOBIN* which is very *RED*, and which contains a lot of *IRON*.
4) *In the lungs, haemoglobin absorbs oxygen* to become *OXYHAEMOGLOBIN*. In body tissues the reverse happens to *release oxygen to the cells*.
5) Red blood cells have *NO NUCLEUS* to *make more room for haemoglobin*.

White Blood Cells

1) Their main role is *DEFENCE AGAINST DISEASE*.
2) They have a *BIG NUCLEUS*.
3) They *GOBBLE UP UNWELCOME MICROBES*.
4) They produce *ANTIBODIES* to fight bacteria.
5) They produce *ANTITOXINS* to neutralise the toxins produced by bacteria.

Plasma

This is a pale straw-coloured liquid which *CARRIES JUST ABOUT EVERYTHING*:
1) *RED* and *WHITE BLOOD CELLS* and *PLATELETS*.
2) Digested food products like *GLUCOSE* and *AMINO ACIDS*.
3) *CARBON DIOXIDE*.
4) *UREA*.
5) *HORMONES*.
6) *ANTIBODIES* and *ANTITOXINS* produced by the white blood cells.

Platelets

1) These are *SMALL FRAGMENTS OF CELLS*.
2) They have *NO NUCLEUS*.
3) They *HELP THE BLOOD TO CLOT* at a wound.
    (So basically they just float about waiting for accidents to happen!)

More Blood, Sweat and Tears...

Do the same as usual — learn the facts *until you can write them down from memory*.

Just in case you think all this formal learning is a waste of time, how do you think you'd get on with these typical Exam questions if you didn't learn it all first?

THREE TYPICAL EXAM QUESTIONS:
1) What is the function of blood plasma? (4 marks)
2) What do white blood cells do? (3 marks)
3) What is the function of haemoglobin? (4 marks)

SECTION TWO — HUMAN BIOLOGY I

Lungs and Breathing

The Thorax

Learn this diagram real good.

1) The *THORAX* is the top part of your 'body'.

2) The *LUNGS* are like *BIG PINK SPONGES*.

3) The *TRACHEA* splits into two tubes called *"BRONCHI"* (each one is "a bronchus"), one going to each lung.

4) The bronchi split into progressively smaller tubes called *BRONCHIOLES*.

5) The bronchioles finally end at small bags called *ALVEOLI* where the gas exchange takes place.

nasal cavity

soft palate

epiglottis

oesophagus (food pipe)

larynx (voicebox)

trachea (wind pipe)

intercostal muscle

bronchiole

bronchus

heart

rib

alveoli

pleural fluid

diaphragm muscle

diaphragm

Breathing In...

1) *Intercostals* and *diaphragm* *CONTRACT*.
2) *Thorax volume* *INCREASES*.
3) Air is *DRAWN IN*.

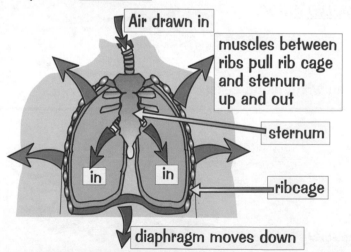

Air drawn in

muscles between ribs pull rib cage and sternum up and out

sternum

in   in

ribcage

diaphragm moves down

...and Breathing Out

1) *Intercostals* and *diaphragm* *RELAX*.
2) *Thorax volume* *DECREASES*.
3) Air is *FORCED OUT*.

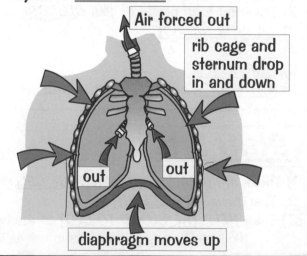

Air forced out

rib cage and sternum drop in and down

out   out

diaphragm moves up

Stop Huffing and Puffing and just LEARN IT...

No dreary lists of facts this time anyway, just three splendid diagrams to learn.
When you practise repeating diagrams from memory, you don't have to draw them really neatly, just sketch them clear enough to label all the important bits. They would never ask you to draw a really fancy diagram in the Exam, but they will expect you to label one. But the only way to be sure you really know a diagram is to sketch it and label it, *all from memory*.

Alveoli, Cells and Diffusion

Alveoli

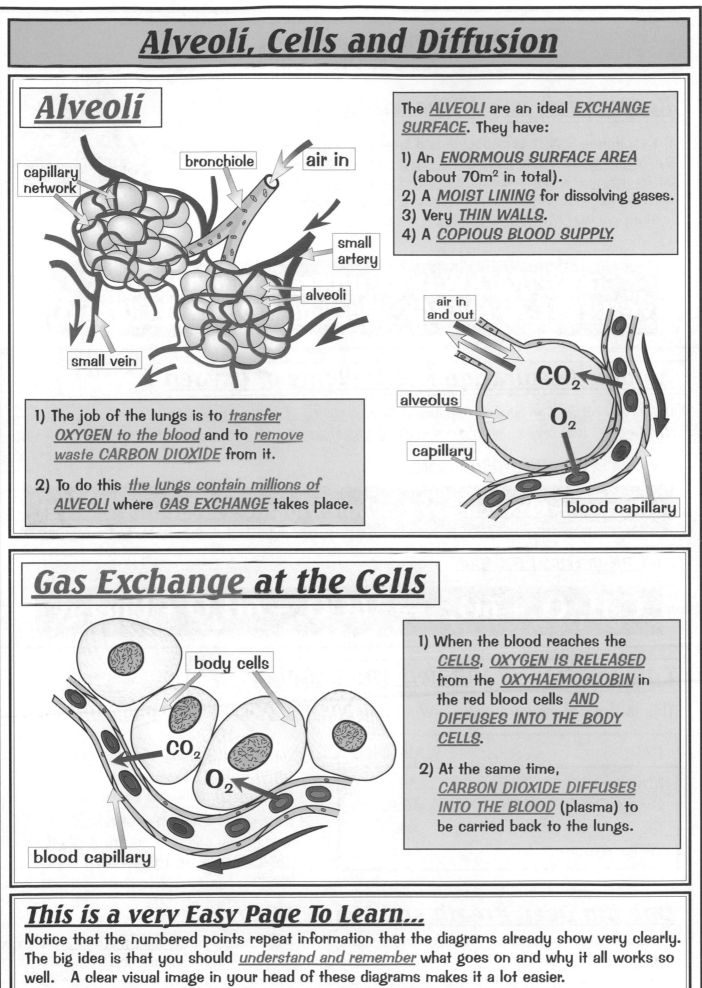

capillary network

bronchiole

air in

small artery

alveoli

small vein

The _ALVEOLI_ are an ideal _EXCHANGE SURFACE_. They have:

1) An _ENORMOUS SURFACE AREA_ (about $70m^2$ in total).
2) A _MOIST LINING_ for dissolving gases.
3) Very _THIN WALLS_.
4) A _COPIOUS BLOOD SUPPLY_.

1) The job of the lungs is to _transfer OXYGEN to the blood_ and to _remove waste CARBON DIOXIDE_ from it.

2) To do this _the lungs contain millions of ALVEOLI_ where _GAS EXCHANGE_ takes place.

air in and out

CO_2

O_2

alveolus

capillary

blood capillary

Gas Exchange at the Cells

body cells

CO_2

O_2

blood capillary

1) When the blood reaches the _CELLS, OXYGEN IS RELEASED_ from the _OXYHAEMOGLOBIN_ in the red blood cells _AND DIFFUSES INTO THE BODY CELLS_.

2) At the same time, _CARBON DIOXIDE DIFFUSES INTO THE BLOOD_ (plasma) to be carried back to the lungs.

This is a very Easy Page To Learn...

Notice that the numbered points repeat information that the diagrams already show very clearly. The big idea is that you should _understand and remember_ what goes on and why it all works so well. A clear visual image in your head of these diagrams makes it a lot easier. _Learn_ the diagrams, words and all, until you can sketch them out _entirely from memory_.

Respiration

Respiration is NOT "breathing in and out"

1) Respiration is NOT breathing in and breathing out, as you might think.
2) _Respiration_ actually goes on _in every cell in your body_.
3) _Respiration_ is the process of _converting glucose to energy_.
4) It takes place in _plants_ too. All living things "_respire_".
   They _convert "food" into energy_.

> ### RESPIRATION is the process of CONVERTING GLUCOSE TO ENERGY, which goes on IN EVERY CELL

Aerobic Respiration Needs Plenty of Oxygen

1) _Aerobic respiration_ is what happens if there's _plenty of oxygen available_.
2) "_Aerobic_" just means "_with air_" and it's _the ideal way to convert glucose into energy_.

You need to learn _THE WORD EQUATION_:

> ### Glucose + Oxygen → Carbon Dioxide + Water + Energy

..and _THE CHEMICAL EQUATION_:

$$C_6H_{12}O_6 + 6O_2 \rightarrow 6CO_2 + 6H_2O + Energy$$

Composition of Inhaled and Exhaled Air

This is the difference between what you _BREATHE IN_ and what you _BREATHE OUT_:

GAS:	AIR IN:	AIR OUT:
Nitrogen	79%	79%
Oxygen	21%	16%
CO_2	0.04%	4%
Water vapour	Varies	Loads

1) Note that the amount of _OXYGEN USED_ matches the amount of _CO_2 PRODUCED_, as in the above equation.

2) Notice that even with millions of alveoli, you still only absorb _A SMALL PROPORTION OF THE OXYGEN_ in each breath.

One Big Deep Breath and LEARN IT...

There are three sections on this page and learning them well enough to _scribble them down_ from _memory_ isn't so difficult. Try to visualise the basic page layout and remember how many numbered points there are for each bit. You don't have to write it out word for word, just make sure you remember the important points about each bit.

Anaerobic Respiration — You and Yeast

Anaerobic Respiration doesn't use Oxygen at all

1) _Anaerobic respiration_ is what happens if there's _no oxygen available_.

2) "Anaerobic" just means "_without_ air" and it's _NOT the best way to convert glucose into energy_.

You need to learn _THE WORD EQUATION_:

> ### Glucose → Energy + Lactic Acid

3) _Anaerobic respiration_ does _not produce nearly as much energy_ as aerobic respiration — but it's useful in emergencies.

Fitness and the Oxygen Debt

1) When you do _vigorous exercise_ and your _body can't supply enough oxygen_ to your muscles they start doing _anaerobic respiration_ instead.

2) _This isn't great_ because _lactic acid builds up_ in the muscles, which gets _painful_.

3) The advantage is that _at least you can keep on using your muscles_ for a while longer.

4) After resorting to anaerobic respiration, when you stop you'll have an _oxygen debt_.

5) In other words _you have to "repay" the oxygen_ which you didn't manage to get to your muscles in time, because _your lungs, heart and blood couldn't keep up with the demand earlier on_.

6) This means you have to _keep breathing hard for a while after you stop_ to get oxygen into your muscles to convert the painful lactic acid to harmless CO_2 and water.

7) When _high levels of CO_2 and lactic acid_ are detected in the blood (by the brain), the _pulse and breathing rate are both increased automatically_ to try and rectify the situation.

8) _A good measure of fitness_ is _how quickly you can recover_ to normal breathing and pulse after doing some vigorous exercise. This is called your _recovery time_.

Anaerobic Respiration in Yeast Makes Bread and Beer

YEAST is used for _MAKING BREAD_ and for _BREWING BEER_, and in both cases the yeast does the business by performing _ANAEROBIC RESPIRATION_.
Another word for this process is _FERMENTATION_. Learn this formula for it:

> ### Glucose → Alcohol + Carbon Dioxide (+ Energy)

In bread-making as the yeast gets to work _it's the CO_2 which makes the bread rise_.
In brewing, of course _the alcohol's the most important bit_, but the CO_2 also makes it kinda fizzy.
(See the Chemistry Book for more details on fermentation.)

Let's See What you Know Then...

Read the page then see what you can _scribble down_ about each of the three sections. _Then try again_. You don't want to try and learn those eight points about "Oxygen Debt" too formally. It's much better to write your own mini-essay on it and then see what stuff you missed. Enjoy.

The Nervous System

Sense Organs and Receptors

THE FIVE SENSE ORGANS ARE:
Eyes   ears   nose   tongue   skin

These five different _sense organs_ all contain different _receptors_.

Receptors are groups of cells which are _sensitive to a stimulus_ such as light or heat, etc.

SENSE ORGANS and RECEPTORS
Don't get them mixed up:

The _EYE_ is a _SENSE ORGAN_ — it contains _LIGHT RECEPTORS_ (rods and cones).
The _EAR_ is a _SENSE ORGAN_ — it contains _SOUND-RECEPTORS_.

RECEPTORS are cells which _TRANSDUCE energy_ (e.g. light energy) into _ELECTRICAL IMPULSES_.

The _FIVE SENSE ORGANS_ and the _stimuli_ that each one is _sensitive to:_

1) EYES
Light receptors.

2) EARS
Sound and _"balance"_ receptors.

3) NOSE
Taste and _smell_ receptors (Chemical stimuli).

4) TONGUE
Taste receptors:
Bitter, salt, sweet and sour (Chemical stimuli).

5) SKIN
Touch, _pressure_ and _temperature_ receptors.

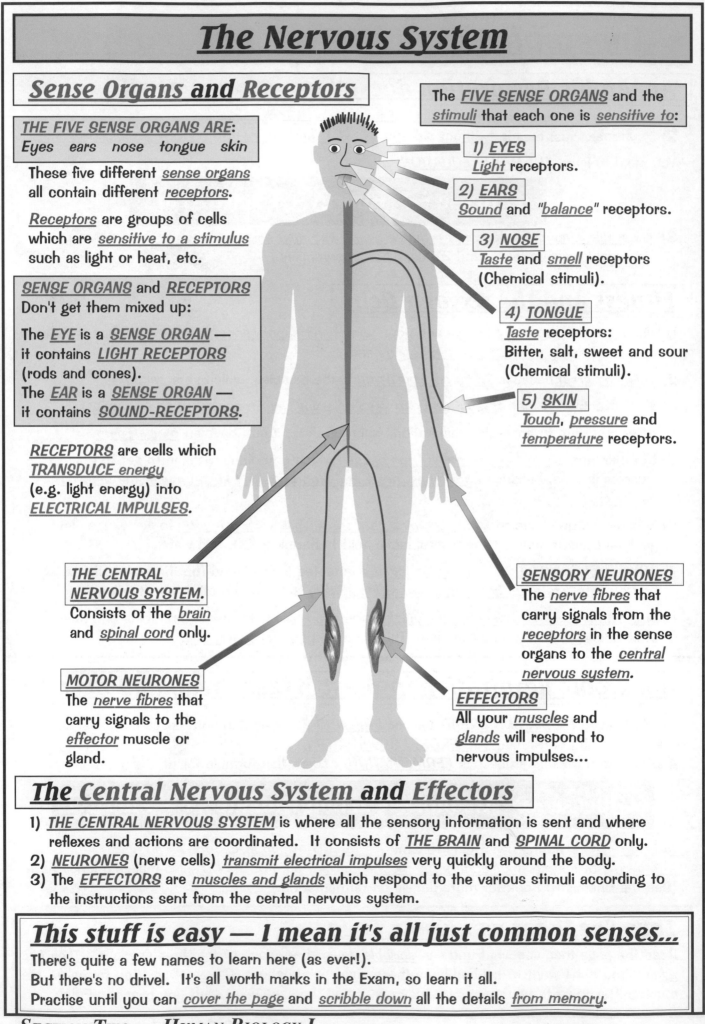

THE CENTRAL NERVOUS SYSTEM.
Consists of the _brain_ and _spinal cord_ only.

MOTOR NEURONES
The _nerve fibres_ that carry signals to the _effector_ muscle or gland.

SENSORY NEURONES
The _nerve fibres_ that carry signals from the _receptors_ in the sense organs to the _central nervous system_.

EFFECTORS
All your _muscles_ and _glands_ will respond to nervous impulses...

The Central Nervous System and Effectors

1) _THE CENTRAL NERVOUS SYSTEM_ is where all the sensory information is sent and where reflexes and actions are coordinated. It consists of _THE BRAIN_ and _SPINAL CORD_ only.
2) _NEURONES_ (nerve cells) _transmit electrical impulses_ very quickly around the body.
3) The _EFFECTORS_ are _muscles and glands_ which respond to the various stimuli according to the instructions sent from the central nervous system.

This stuff is easy — I mean it's all just common senses...

There's quite a few names to learn here (as ever!).
But there's no drivel. It's all worth marks in the Exam, so learn it all.
Practise until you can _cover the page_ and _scribble down_ all the details _from memory_.

Neurones and Reflexes

The Three Types of Neurone are All Much The Same

The THREE TYPES of NEURONE are:

(They're all *pretty much the same*, they're just *connected to different things*, that's all.)

1) *SENSORY neurone*,
2) *MOTOR neurone*
3) *RELAY neurone* (or *CONNECTOR neurone*).

A Typical Neurone: — *Learn the names* of all the bits:

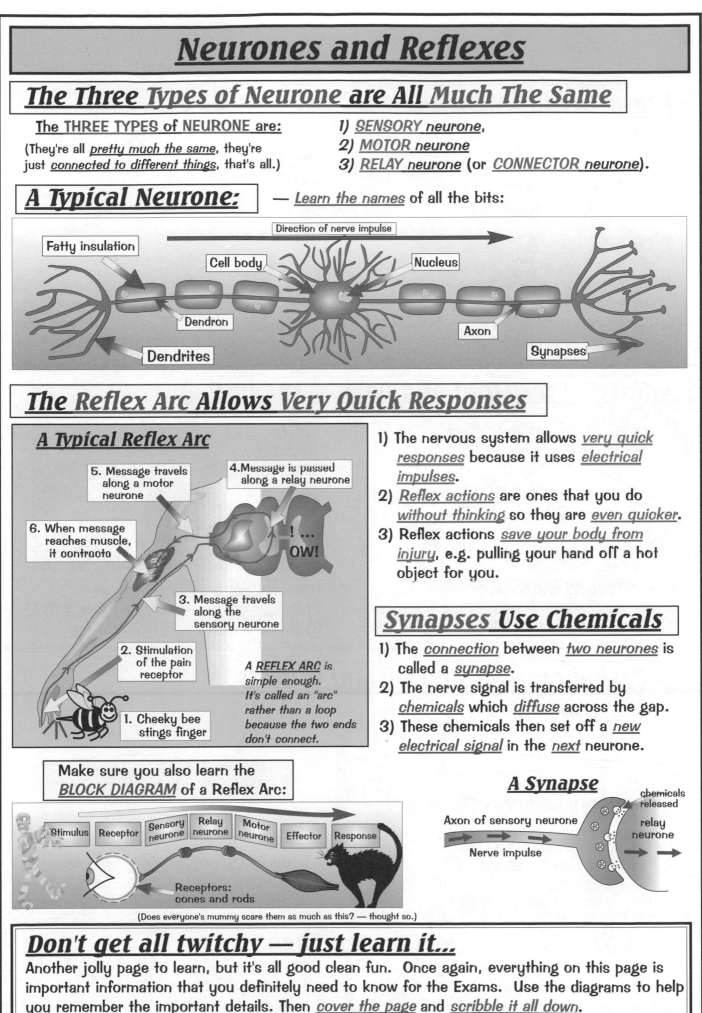

Direction of nerve impulse

Fatty insulation

Cell body

Nucleus

Dendron

Axon

Dendrites

Synapses

The Reflex Arc Allows Very Quick Responses

A Typical Reflex Arc

5. Message travels along a motor neurone

4. Message is passed along a relay neurone

6. When message reaches muscle, it contracts

! ... OW!

3. Message travels along the sensory neurone

2. Stimulation of the pain receptor

A *REFLEX ARC* is simple enough. It's called an "arc" rather than a loop because the two ends don't connect.

1. Cheeky bee stings finger

1) The nervous system allows *very quick responses* because it uses *electrical impulses*.
2) *Reflex actions* are ones that you do *without thinking* so they are *even quicker*.
3) Reflex actions *save your body from injury*, e.g. pulling your hand off a hot object for you.

Synapses Use Chemicals

1) The *connection* between *two neurones* is called a *synapse*.
2) The nerve signal is transferred by *chemicals* which *diffuse* across the gap.
3) These chemicals then set off a *new electrical signal* in the *next* neurone.

Make sure you also learn the *BLOCK DIAGRAM* of a Reflex Arc:

Stimulus | Receptor | Sensory neurone | Relay neurone | Motor neurone | Effector | Response

Receptors: cones and rods

(Does everyone's mummy scare them as much as this? — thought so.)

A Synapse

chemicals released

Axon of sensory neurone

relay neurone

Nerve impulse

Don't get all twitchy — just learn it...

Another jolly page to learn, but it's all good clean fun. Once again, everything on this page is important information that you definitely need to know for the Exams. Use the diagrams to help you remember the important details. Then *cover the page* and *scribble it all down*.

The Eye

Learn The Eye with all its labels:

1) The *pupil* is the *hole* in the middle of the iris, which *the light goes through*.
2) The *aqueous humour* is a *clear liquid* and the *vitreous humour* is a *clear jelly*. They *support* the spherical shape of the eye.
3) The *retina* is the *light sensitive* part and is covered in *rods and cones*.
4) *Rods* are more sensitive in *dim light* but only sense in *black and white*.
5) *Cones* are sensitive to *colours* but are not so good in dim light.

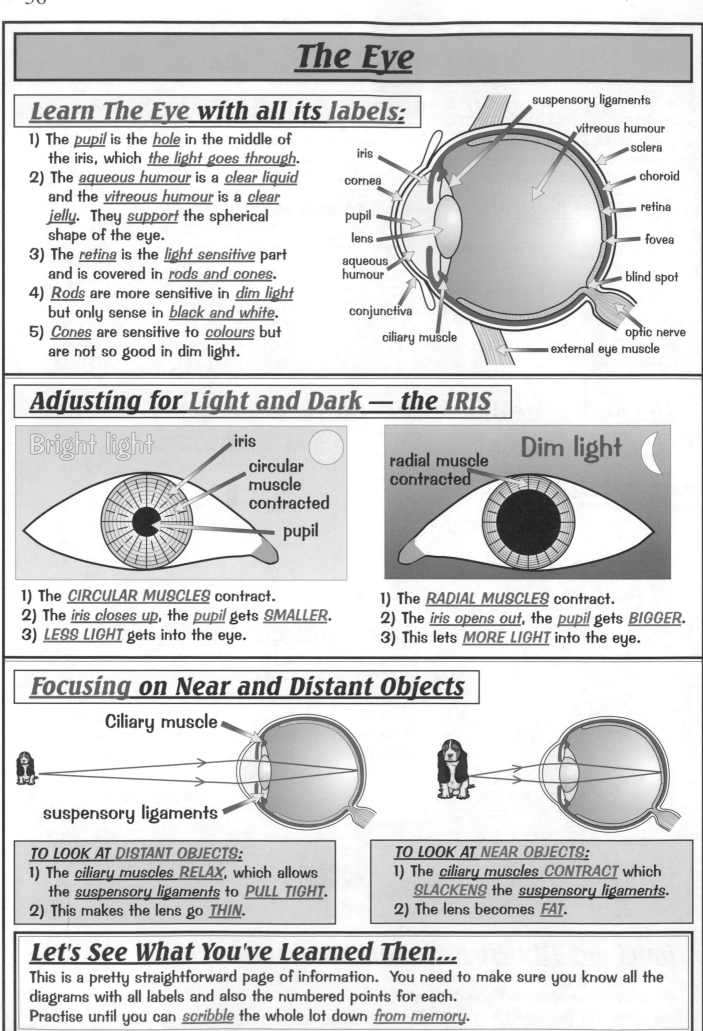

suspensory ligaments
vitreous humour
sclera
choroid
retina
fovea
blind spot
optic nerve
external eye muscle
iris
cornea
pupil
lens
aqueous humour
conjunctiva
ciliary muscle

Adjusting for Light and Dark — the IRIS

Bright light

iris
circular muscle contracted
pupil

1) The *CIRCULAR MUSCLES* contract.
2) The *iris closes up*, the *pupil* gets *SMALLER*.
3) *LESS LIGHT* gets into the eye.

Dim light

radial muscle contracted

1) The *RADIAL MUSCLES* contract.
2) The *iris opens out*, the *pupil* gets *BIGGER*.
3) This lets *MORE LIGHT* into the eye.

Focusing on Near and Distant Objects

Ciliary muscle

suspensory ligaments

TO LOOK AT DISTANT OBJECTS:
1) The *ciliary muscles RELAX*, which allows the *suspensory ligaments* to *PULL TIGHT*.
2) This makes the lens go *THIN*.

TO LOOK AT NEAR OBJECTS:
1) The *ciliary muscles CONTRACT* which *SLACKENS* the *suspensory ligaments*.
2) The lens becomes *FAT*.

Let's See What You've Learned Then...

This is a pretty straightforward page of information. You need to make sure you know all the diagrams with all labels and also the numbered points for each.
Practise until you can *scribble* the whole lot down *from memory*.

Revision Summary for Section Two

Phew, there's a lot of stuff to learn in Section Two. And it's all that grisly "open heart surgery" type stuff too, with all those gory diagrams. Mind you, it's all fairly straightforward and factual — you know, nothing difficult to understand, just lots of facts to learn. And lots of gory diagrams. You know the big plan with these questions though. Keep practising till you can whizz them all off without a moment's hesitation on any of them. It's a nice trick if you can do it.

1) Write down the seven types of nutrient needed in a balanced diet.
2) Say what kind of foods each one is found in, and what the nutrient is needed for.
3) Sketch a diagram of the digestive system and put the ten labels on it.
4) Write down at least two details for each of the ten labelled parts.
5) What *exactly* do enzymes do in the digestive system?
6) List the three main digestive enzymes, which foods they act on, and what they produce.
7) What *two* things does bile do? Where is it produced? Where does it enter the system?
8) Draw a full diagram of a single tooth, and one of the jaw showing all four types of teeth.
9) Draw a diagram of a peristaltic squeeze and label the different types of tissue, with their use.
10) Sketch a villus, and say what it's for. Point out the three main features of villi.
11) What are the three "big" food molecules, and which kind of foods are each of them found in?
12) What small molecules are they each broken down into in the digestive system?
13) Sketch a diagram showing what then happens to the small molecules.
14) Describe the symptoms of a lack of: a) protein b) iron c) calcium d) vitamin C e) vitamin D.
15) Detail the four boring food tests: a) starch b) protein c) simple sugars d) fats.
16) Draw a diagram of the human circulatory system: heart, lungs, arteries, veins, etc.
17) Explain why it is a *double* circulatory system, and describe the pressure and oxygen content of the blood in each bit. What are the big words for saying if the blood has oxygen in or not?
18) Draw a full diagram of the heart with all the labels. Explain how the two halves differ.
19) How do ventricles and atria compare, and why? What are the valves for?
20) Describe briefly with diagrams the three stages of the pumping cycle for the heart.
21) Sketch an artery, a capillary, and a vein, with labels, and explain the features of all three.
22) Sketch a red blood cell and a white blood cell and give five details about each.
23) Sketch some blood plasma. List all the things that are carried in the plasma (around 10).
24) Sketch some platelets. What do they do all day?
25) Draw a diagram of the thorax, showing all the breathing equipment.
26) Describe what happens during breathing in and breathing out. Be sure to give all the details.
27) Where are alveoli found? How big are they and what are they for? Give four features.
28) Explain what happens to oxygen and carbon dioxide, both at alveoli and at body cells.
29) What is respiration? Give a proper definition.
30) What is the composition of inhaled and exhaled air? Give two comments on the difference.
31) What is "aerobic respiration"? Give the word and symbol equations for it.
32) What is "anaerobic respiration"? Give the word equation for what happens in our bodies.
33) Explain about fitness and the oxygen debt.
34) What is the word equation for fermentation? What two products use fermentation?
35) Draw a diagram showing the main parts of the nervous system.
36) List the five sense organs and say what kind of receptors each one has.
37) What are effectors? What two things constitute the central nervous system?
38) What are the three types of neurone? Draw a detailed diagram of a typical neurone.
39) Describe how a reflex arc works and why it's a good thing. Explain how a synapse works.
40) Draw a full diagram of an eye with all labels and details.
41) Describe how the eye adjusts for light and dark, and to focus on near and distant objects.

Hormones

Hormones are Chemical Messengers sent in the Blood

1) Hormones are *CHEMICALS* released *DIRECTLY INTO THE BLOOD*.
2) They are carried in the *BLOOD PLASMA* to other parts of the body.
3) They are produced in various *GLANDS* (endocrine glands) as shown on the diagram.
4) They *TRAVEL ALL OVER THE BODY* but only affect *PARTICULAR CELLS* in particular places.
5) The cells they affect are called *TARGET CELLS*.
6) They travel at *"THE SPEED OF BLOOD"*.
7) They have *LONG-LASTING EFFECTS*.
8) They control things that need *CONSTANT ADJUSTMENT*.

LEARN THIS DEFINITION:

HORMONES ...
are *chemical messengers*
which *travel in the blood*
to *activate target cells*.

THE PITUITARY GLAND

This produces many important hormones: *LH*, *FSH* and *ADH*
These tend to *control other glands*, as a rule.

ADRENAL GLAND

Produces *adrenaline* which prepares the body with the well known *fight or flight* reaction:
Increased *blood sugar*, *heart rate*, *breathing rate*, and *diversion of blood* from skin to muscles.

PANCREAS

Produces *insulin* for the control of *blood sugar*
(If you're doing NEAB it also produces *glucagon*).

Kidney

OVARIES — females only

Produce *oestrogen* which promotes all *female secondary sexual characteristics* during puberty:
1) *Extra hair* in places.
2) Changes in body *proportions*.
3) *Egg* production.

TESTES — males only

Produce *testosterone* which promotes all *male secondary sexual characteristics* at puberty:
1) *Extra hair* in places.
2) Changes in body *proportions*.
3) *Sperm* production.

Hormones and Nerves do Similar Jobs, but there are Important Differences

NERVES:
1) Very *FAST* message.
2) Act for a very *SHORT TIME*.
3) Act on a very *PRECISE AREA*.
4) *IMMEDIATE* reaction.

HORMONES:
1) *SLOWER* message.
2) Act for a *LONG TIME*.
3) Act in a more *GENERAL* way.
4) *LONGER-TERM* reaction.

Hormones — Easy peasy...

Well let's face it, there's not much to learn here is there? The diagram and all its labels are easy enough, and so's the comparison of nerves and hormones. The definition of hormones is worth learning word for word. The eight points at the top of the page are best done with the good old "*mini-essay*" method. *Learn it*, *cover the page* and *scribble*. Then *try again*. And smile of course.

Insulin and Diabetes

Insulin is a _hormone_ which controls how much _sugar_ there is in your _blood_. **LEARN** how it does it:

Insulin Controls Blood Sugar Levels

1) Eating _carbohydrate_ foods puts a lot of _glucose_ into the blood from the _gut_.
2) _Normal metabolism_ of cells _removes glucose_ from the blood.
3) Vigorous _exercise_ removes _much more_ glucose from the blood.
4) Obviously, to keep the _level_ of blood glucose _controlled_ there has to be a way to _add or remove_ glucose from the blood.   And this is it:

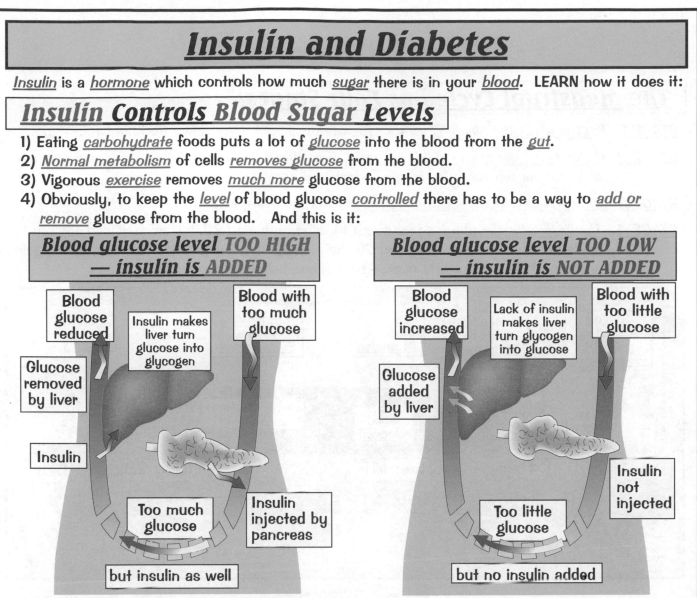

Blood glucose level _TOO HIGH_ — insulin is _ADDED_

Blood glucose reduced

Insulin makes liver turn glucose into glycogen

Blood with too much glucose

Glucose removed by liver

Insulin

Too much glucose

Insulin injected by pancreas

but insulin as well

Blood glucose level _TOO LOW_ — insulin is _NOT ADDED_

Blood glucose increased

Lack of insulin makes liver turn glycogen into glucose

Blood with too little glucose

Glucose added by liver

Insulin not injected

Too little glucose

but no insulin added

Remember, the _addition_ of insulin _reduces_ blood sugar level.
(For _NEAB syllabuses_ you also need to know that when the blood sugar is _too low_, another hormone called _Glucagon_ is added instead of insulin. Glucagon makes the liver _release glucose_ into the blood.)

Diabetes — the Pancreas Stops Making Enough Insulin

1) _Diabetes is a disease_ in which _the pancreas doesn't produce enough insulin_.
2) The result is that a person's _blood sugar can rise to a level that can kill them_.
3) The problem can be _controlled_ in _two ways_:

A) _Avoiding foods rich in carbohydrate_ (which turns to glucose when digested).
   It can also be helpful to take _exercise_ after eating carbohydrates... i.e. trying to _use up_ the _extra glucose_ by doing _physical activity_, but this isn't usually very practical.

B) _INJECTING INSULIN INTO THE BLOOD_ before meals, (especially if high in carbohydrates).
   This will make the liver _remove the glucose_ from the blood _as soon as it enters it_ from the gut, when the (carbohydrate-rich) food is being _digested_.   This stops the level of glucose in the blood from getting too high and is a _very effective treatment_.

Learn all this stuff about blood sugar and diabetes...

This stuff on blood sugar and insulin can seem a bit confusing at first, but if you concentrate on learning those two diagrams, it'll all start to get a lot easier. Don't forget that only carbohydrate foods put the blood sugar levels up. _Learn it all_, then _cover the page_ and _scribble it all down_.

SECTION THREE — HUMAN BIOLOGY II

Female Menstrual Cycle

The Menstrual Cycle has Four Stages

STAGE 1 *Day 1 is when the bleeding starts*. The uterus lining breaks down for about four days.

STAGE 2 *The lining of the womb builds up again*, from day 4 to day 14, into a thick spongy layer of blood vessels ready to receive a fertilised egg.

STAGE 3 *An egg is developed and then released* from the ovary at day 14.

STAGE 4 *The wall is then maintained* for about 14 days, until day 28. If no fertilised egg has landed on the uterus wall by day 28 then the spongy lining starts to break down again and the whole cycle starts over. The diagram below illustrates this.

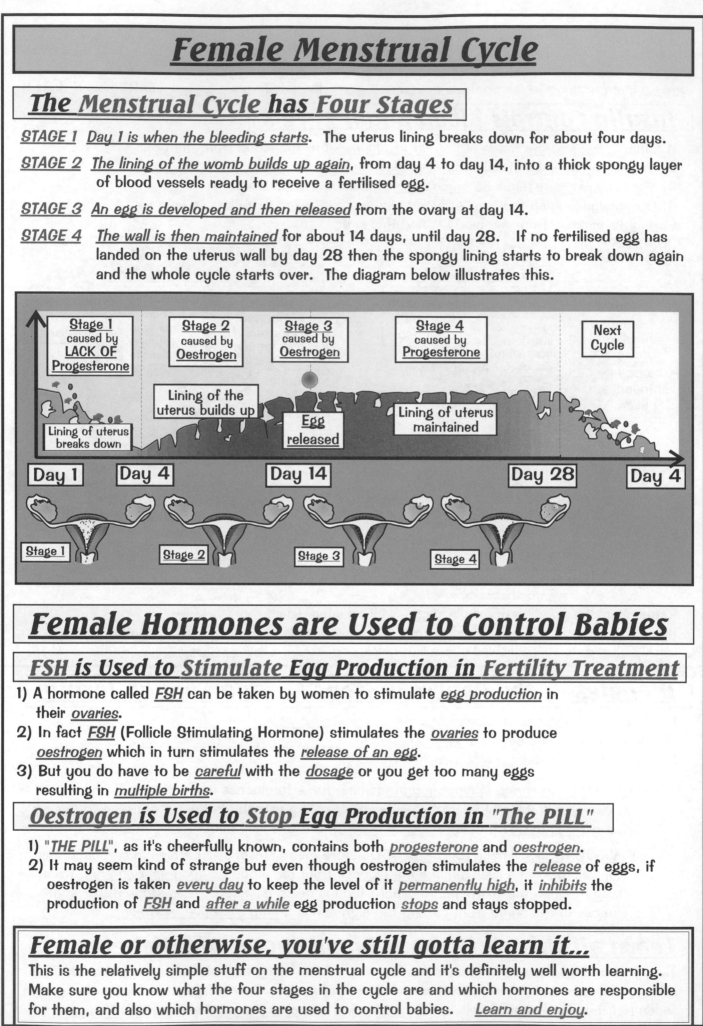

Female Hormones are Used to Control Babies

FSH is Used to Stimulate Egg Production in Fertility Treatment

1) A hormone called *FSH* can be taken by women to stimulate *egg production* in their *ovaries*.
2) In fact *FSH* (Follicle Stimulating Hormone) stimulates the *ovaries* to produce *oestrogen* which in turn stimulates the *release of an egg*.
3) But you do have to be *careful* with the *dosage* or you get too many eggs resulting in *multiple births*.

Oestrogen is Used to Stop Egg Production in "The PILL"

1) "*THE PILL*", as it's cheerfully known, contains both *progesterone* and *oestrogen*.
2) It may seem kind of strange but even though oestrogen stimulates the *release* of eggs, if oestrogen is taken *every day* to keep the level of it *permanently high*, it *inhibits* the production of *FSH* and *after a while* egg production *stops* and stays stopped.

Female or otherwise, you've still gotta learn it...

This is the relatively simple stuff on the menstrual cycle and it's definitely well worth learning. Make sure you know what the four stages in the cycle are and which hormones are responsible for them, and also which hormones are used to control babies. *Learn and enjoy.*

Hormones in the Menstrual Cycle

Oestrogen and Progesterone are The Two Main Hormones

These two hormones are produced in the _ovaries_ and they control the main events of the cycle:

1) OESTROGEN:
    1) Causes the _lining of the uterus_ to _thicken_ and _grow_.
    2) Stimulates the _release of an egg_ at day 14.

2) PROGESTERONE:
    1) _Maintains the lining_ of the uterus.
       When the level of progesterone _falls_, the lining _breaks down_.

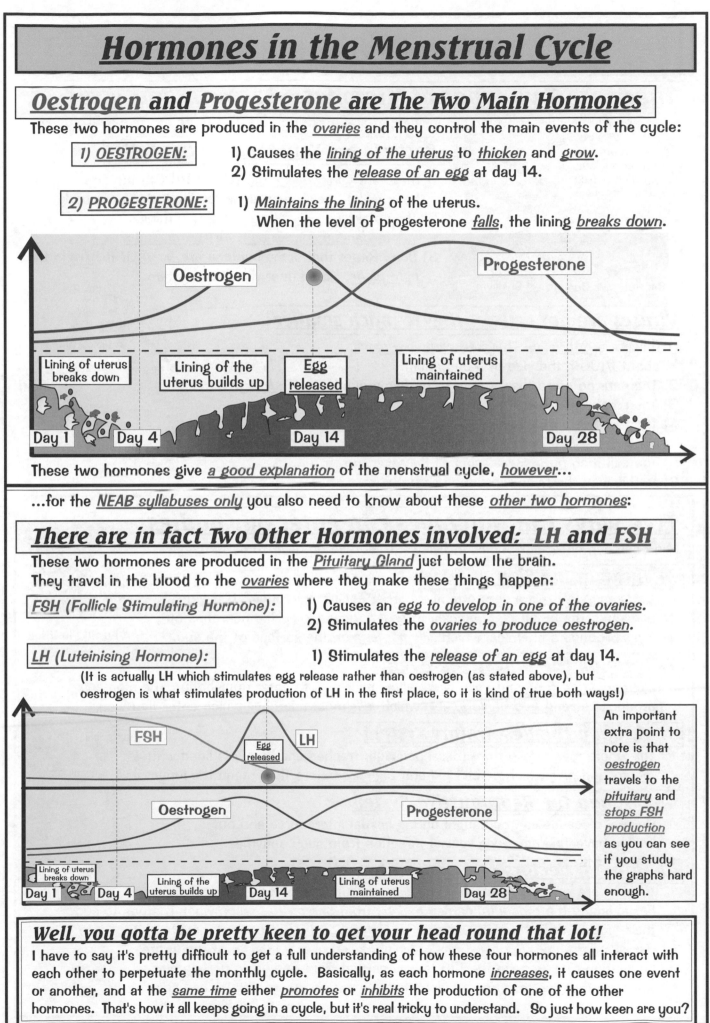

These two hormones give _a good explanation_ of the menstrual cycle, _however_...

...for the _NEAB syllabuses only_ you also need to know about these _other two hormones_:

There are in fact Two Other Hormones involved: LH and FSH

These two hormones are produced in the _Pituitary Gland_ just below the brain.
They travel in the blood to the _ovaries_ where they make these things happen:

FSH (Follicle Stimulating Hormone):
    1) Causes an _egg to develop in one of the ovaries_.
    2) Stimulates the _ovaries to produce oestrogen_.

LH (Luteinising Hormone):
    1) Stimulates the _release of an egg_ at day 14.

(It is actually LH which stimulates egg release rather than oestrogen (as stated above), but oestrogen is what stimulates production of LH in the first place, so it is kind of true both ways!)

An important extra point to note is that _oestrogen_ travels to the _pituitary_ and _stops FSH production_ as you can see if you study the graphs hard enough.

Well, you gotta be pretty keen to get your head round that lot!

I have to say it's pretty difficult to get a full understanding of how these four hormones all interact with each other to perpetuate the monthly cycle. Basically, as each hormone _increases_, it causes one event or another, and at the _same time_ either _promotes_ or _inhibits_ the production of one of the other hormones. That's how it all keeps going in a cycle, but it's real tricky to understand. So just how keen are you?

SECTION THREE — HUMAN BIOLOGY II

Disease in Humans

There are Two types of Microbes: Bacteria and Viruses

Microbes are organisms which get inside you and make you feel ill. There are two main types:

Bacteria are cells with no nucleus. The DNA is free in the cytoplasm

Bacillus   Coccus   Spirillum

Bacteria are Very Small Living Cells

1) These are _very small cells_, (about 1/100th the size of your body cells), which reproduce rapidly inside your body.
2) They make you _feel ill_ by doing _two_ things:
   a) _damaging your cells_   b) _producing toxins_.
3) Don't forget that some bacteria are _useful_ if they're in the _right place_, like in your digestive system.

string of DNA
protein coat

A typical virus

Viruses are not cells — they're much smaller

1) These are _not cells_. They are _very very small_, about 1/100th the size of a bacterium.
2) They are no more than a _coat of protein_ around a _DNA strand_.
3) They make you feel ill by _damaging your cells_.
4) They _replicate themselves_ by invading the _nucleus_ of a cell and using the _DNA_ it contains to produce many _copies_ of themselves.
5) The cell then _bursts_, releasing all the new viruses.
6) In this way they can reproduce _very quickly_.

eek!

Five ways that microbes can enter our bodies

Microbes can enter our bodies in five ways, but we do have some _defences_.

A horrid Flu Virus

1) Through the Skin and Eyes

Undamaged skin is a very effective barrier against microbes. If it gets damaged, the blood _clots_ quickly to _seal cuts_ and keep the microbes out. _Eyes_ produce a chemical which _kills bacteria_ on the surface of the eye.

2) Through the Digestive System

Contaminated food and _dirty water_ allow microbes to enter your body. The stomach produces strong _hydrochloric acid_ which _kills_ most microbes which enter that way.

3) Through the Respiratory System

The whole _respiratory tract_ (nasal passage, trachea and lungs) is lined with _mucus_ and _cilia_ which catch _dust_ and _bacteria_ before they reach the lungs.

cilia
mucus
nucleus

4) Through the Reproductive System

Several diseases can be caught during sexual intercourse and our bodies have _few defences_ against infection from such activities.

goblet cell

5) Through Vectors (e.g. mosquitos, fleas)

Vectors are _organisms_ which _carry disease_ from one person to another. For example the _mosquito_ carries _malaria_ from _person to person_ when it stops to suck their _blood_. Unfortunately we have _no natural protection_ against insects _spitting_ into our _bloodstream_. _The black death_, which killed over _a quarter_ of the entire population of _Europe_ in the 1300s was carried from _person to person_ by the _fleas_ that live on _rats_. We don't tolerate rats any more, they're bad news.

(Apart from Adele's pet ones)

Fighting Disease

Once microbes have entered our bodies they will _reproduce rapidly_ unless they are _destroyed_. Your '_immune system_' does just that, and _white blood cells_ are the most important part of it.

Your Immune System: White blood cells

They _travel around_ in your blood and _crawl into every part of you_, constantly _patrolling_ for microbes. When they come across an invading _microbe_ they have _three lines of attack_:

1) Consuming Them

White blood cells can _engulf_ foreign cells and _digest_ them.

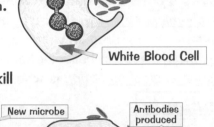

microbes

White Blood Cell

2) Producing Antibodies

When your white blood cells come across a _foreign cell_ they will _start to produce_ chemicals called _antibodies_ to kill the new invading cells. The antibodies are then produced _rapidly_ and flow _all round the body_ to kill all _similar_ bacteria or viruses.

New microbe

Antibodies produced

New microbes attacked by new antibodies

3) Producing Antitoxins

Antitoxins counter the effect of any _poisons_ (toxins) produced by the _invading bacteria_.

Immunisation — producing antibodies beforehand

1) Once your _white cells_ have produced _antibodies_ to tackle a _new strain_ of bacteria or virus you are said to have developed "_natural immunity_" to it.
2) That means if you get infected by the _same microbes_ in future they'll be killed _immediately_ by the _antibodies_ you already have for them, and you _won't get ill_.
3) The trouble is when a _new_ microbe appears, it takes your white cells _a few days_ to produce the antibodies to deal with them and in that time you can get _very ill_.
4) There are _plenty of diseases_ which can make you _very ill indeed_ (e.g. polio, tetanus, measles) and only _immunisation_ stops you getting them.
5) Immunisation involves injecting _dead microbes_ into you. This causes your body to produce _antibodies_ to them, even though they're dead. They can do no _harm_ to you because they're dead.
6) If _live microbes of the same type_ appeared _after that_ however, they'd be _killed immediately_ before they could do you any harm.

Antibiotics kill Bacteria but NOT Viruses

1) _Antibiotics_ are _drugs_ that kill _bacteria_ without killing your own body cells.
2) They are _very useful_ for clearing up infections that your body is having _trouble_ with.
3) However they don't kill _viruses_. _Flu and colds_ are caused by _viruses_ and basically, _you're on your own_, pal.
4) There are _no drugs_ to kill _viruses_ and you just have to _wait_ for your body to deal with it and _suffer_ in the meantime.
5) Still, it's better than being bitten by a rat flea.

A horrid Flu Virus   An even more horrid Rat Flea

It's Grisly Stuff, but worth learning just the Same...

Two pages this time, and definitely 'mini-essay' material. There are four main sections, with several subsections. Do a _mini-essay_ on each subsection and then _check_ what you forgot.

<u>Drugs</u>

1) Drugs are substances which alter the way the body works. Some drugs are useful of course, for example antibiotics such as penicillin. However there are many drugs which are <u>dangerous</u> if misused, and many of them are <u>addictive</u> or "habit-forming".
2) The loss of control and judgement caused by many drugs can easily lead to <u>death</u> from various other causes, e.g. choking on vomit, falling down stairs, passing under vehicles, etc.

<u>There are two types of Addiction — Chemical and Psychological</u>

1) There's a difference between true chemical addiction and just psychological addiction.
2) In <u>chemical addiction</u> the body becomes adjusted to the constant presence of the drug in the system. If the drug is withdrawn, there are various <u>unpleasant physical withdrawal symptoms</u>: fevers, hallucinations, nausea, and the shakes.
3) <u>Psychological addiction</u> is where the person "feels the need" to keep taking the drug.

<u>Stimulants</u>

1) Stimulants tend to make the nervous system generally more alert and "awake".
2) Caffeine is a mild stimulant found in tea and coffee. It's pretty harmless. Few lives are wrecked by obsessive tea-drinking.
3) However, amphetamine and methedrine are also stimulants.
4) Strong stimulants like these produce a feeling of boundless energy, but the person experiences <u>serious depression</u> if they stop taking it, so an unhealthy <u>dependence</u> develops all too easily. Continued use can lead to hallucinations and <u>changes in personality</u>.

<u>Hallucinogens — LSD and Ecstasy</u>

1) LSD is hallucinogenic, i.e. it causes hallucinations.
2) Ecstasy is hallucinogenic in high doses, but in smaller amounts gives a feeling of boundless energy similar to that from amphetamines, together with the same <u>serious problem</u> of a growing <u>dependence</u>.
3) The feeling of energy leads to a <u>danger of overheating</u> and <u>collapse</u> through <u>dehydration</u>.

<u>Depressants slow down your responses — Alcohol and Barbiturates</u>

Depressants tend to slow down the responses of the nervous system, causing <u>slow reactions</u> and poor judgement of speed, distances, etc. See "Alcohol" on the next page.

<u>Pain Killers — Aspirin, Heroin and Morphine</u>

1) Heroin is a <u>particularly nasty</u> drug causing a serious <u>deterioration</u> in personality and as the addiction grows the person's whole life <u>degenerates</u> into a <u>desperate struggle</u> to obtain money for their daily heroin requirement, often resulting in a <u>sad life of crime</u> to pay for it.
2) Morphine is also highly <u>addictive</u>.
3) Aspirin is a useful painkiller for many minor illnesses, but its overuse has <u>harmful effects</u>.

<u>Solvents</u>

1) Solvents are found in a variety of "household" items e.g. glues, paints etc.
2) They are <u>dangerous</u> and have many <u>damaging effects</u> on your body and personality.
3) They cause hallucinations and adversely affect personality and behaviour.
4) They cause <u>damage</u> to the <u>lungs</u>, <u>brain</u>, <u>liver</u> and <u>kidney</u>.

<u>Learn about these drugs and then forget them...</u>

Anyone with half a brain avoids these drugs like they do <u>rat fleas</u>.
Enjoy your life, instead of being a sucker.

Alcohol and Tobacco

1) Alcohol and tobacco are the two main (non-medical) drugs which are legal in this country.

2) But don't be fooled. They can do you a lot of _harm_ just like the other drugs can.

Alcohol

1) The main effect of alcohol is to reduce the activity of the nervous system. The positive aspect of this is that it makes us feel less inhibited, and there's no doubt that alcohol in moderation helps people to socialise and relax with each other.

2) However, if you let alcohol take over, _it can wreck your life_. And it does. It wrecks a lot of people's lives. You've got to control it.

3) Once alcohol starts to take over someone's life there are many _harmful effects_:

   a) Alcohol is basically _poisonous_. Too much drinking will cause _severe damage_ to the _liver_ and the _brain_ leading to _liver disease_ and a noticeable _drop_ in brain function.

   b) Too much alcohol _impairs judgement_ which can cause accidents, and it can also severely affect the person's work and home life.

   c) _Serious dependency on alcohol_ can eventually lead to _loss of job_, _loss of income_ and the start of a _severe downward spiral_.

Smoking Tobacco

Smoking is no good to anyone. It doesn't have any positive social aspects and is _without any doubt at all a very serious cause of ill health_.

And once you've started smoking _there's no going back_. It's a one way trip pal.

And you'll notice that smokers are _no happier_ than non smokers, _even when they're smoking_. What may start off as something "different" to do, rapidly becomes something they _have_ to do, just to feel OK. But non-smokers feel just as OK _without_ spending £20 or more each week and _wrecking their health_ into the bargain.

And why do people start smoking? To look the part, that's why. They have an image in their head of how they want to appear and smoking seems the perfect _fashion accessory_.

Well just remember, _it's a one way trip_. You might think it makes you look cool at 16, but will it still seem the perfect fashion accessory when you're 20 with a new group of friends who don't smoke? Nope. Too late. You're stuck with it.

And by the time you're 60 it'll have cost you over £40,000. Enough to buy a Ferrari or a new house. That's quite an expensive fashion accessory.

Smoking? Cool? Oh yeah — it's about as cool as cool can be, I'd say.

Oh and by the way...

Tobacco smoke does this inside your body:

1) It _coats_ the _inside of your lungs_ with tar so they become _hideously inefficient_.

2) It covers the cilia in _tar_ preventing them from getting bacteria out of your lungs.

3) It causes _disease_ of the _heart_ and _blood vessels_, leading to _heart attacks_ and _strokes_.

4) It causes _lung cancer_. Out of every _ten_ lung cancer patients, _nine_ of them smoke.

5) It causes _severe_ loss of lung function leading to diseases like _emphysema_ and _bronchitis_, in which the inside of the lungs is basically _wrecked_. People with severe bronchitis can't manage even a brisk walk, because their lungs can't get enough oxygen into the blood. It eventually _kills_ over _20,000 people_ in Britain every year.

6) But this is the best bit. The effect of the nicotine is _negligible_ — other than to make you _addicted_ to it. It doesn't make you high — just _dependent_. Great. Fantastic.

Learn the Numbered Points for your Exam...

It's the disease aspects they concentrate on most in the Exams. Learn the rest for a nice life.

Homeostasis

Homeostasis is a fancy word. It covers lot of things, so I guess it has to be. Homeostasis covers all the functions of your body which try to maintain a "*constant internal environment*". Learn the definition:

HOMEOSTASIS — *the maintenance of a CONSTANT INTERNAL ENVIRONMENT*

There are *six different bodily levels* that need to be controlled:

1) REMOVAL OF CO_2
2) REMOVAL OF *UREA*
3) *ION* content
4) *WATER* content
5) *SUGAR* content
6) *TEMPERATURE*

⟸ These two are *WASTES*. They're constantly produced in the body and *you just need to get rid of them*.

⟸ These four are all *"GOODIES"* and we need them, *BUT AT JUST THE RIGHT LEVEL* — not too much and not too little.

All your body's cells are *BATHED IN TISSUE FLUID*, which is just *blood plasma* which has leaked out of the capillaries (on purpose).

To keep all your cells working properly, *this fluid must be just right* — in other words, *THE SIX THINGS* above must be *KEPT AT THE RIGHT LEVEL* — not too high, and not too low.

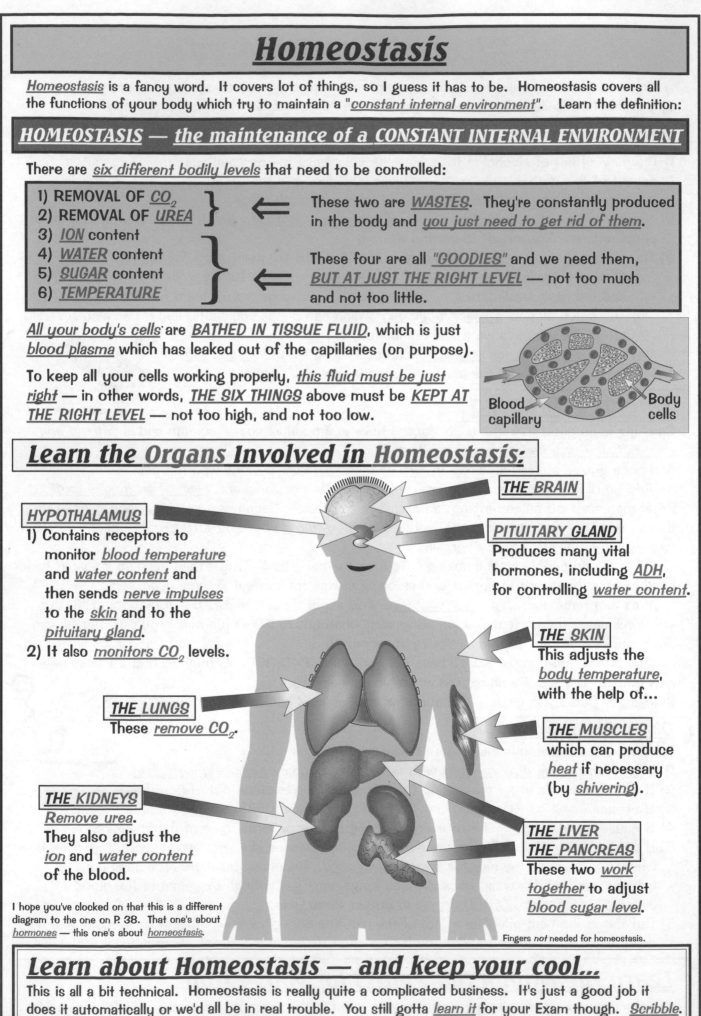

Blood capillary

Body cells

Learn the Organs Involved in Homeostasis:

THE BRAIN

HYPOTHALAMUS
1) Contains receptors to monitor *blood temperature* and *water content* and then sends *nerve impulses* to the *skin* and to the *pituitary gland*.
2) It also *monitors CO_2* levels.

PITUITARY GLAND
Produces many vital hormones, including *ADH*, for controlling *water content*.

THE SKIN
This adjusts the *body temperature*, with the help of...

THE LUNGS
These *remove CO_2*.

THE MUSCLES
which can produce *heat* if necessary (by *shivering*).

THE KIDNEYS
Remove urea.
They also adjust the *ion* and *water content* of the blood.

THE LIVER THE PANCREAS
These two *work together* to adjust *blood sugar level*.

I hope you've clocked on that this is a different diagram to the one on P. 38. That one's about *hormones* — this one's about *homeostasis*.

Fingers *not* needed for homeostasis.

Learn about Homeostasis — and keep your cool...

This is all a bit technical. Homeostasis is really quite a complicated business. It's just a good job it does it automatically or we'd all be in real trouble. You still gotta *learn it* for your Exam though. *Scribble*.

Skin

Well, talk about *"maintaining a constant internal environment"* (as you do). It'd be pretty tricky without *skin* wouldn't it.

There are Three Main Things that Skin does for you:

> 1) It stops you *DRYING UP* (*DEHYDRATING*).
> 2) It keeps *GERMS OUT*.
> 3) It helps control your *TEMPERATURE*.

The first two are really pretty obvious. The skin is a waterproof, germproof, nearly-everything-that's-not-too-sharp-or-hot-or-moving-too-fast-proof layer that keeps the rest of the world out and so maintains your precious *"constant internal environment"* so all your little cells can carry on their daily business in warmth and comfort.

(This is starting to remind me of a school, with you lot as the cells, being kept warm, well fed, freshly watered, and constantly supplied with all the stuff you need to carry on your daily 'work'— gee, it's kinda like "Homeostasis High".)

The Skin has Three Tricks for Altering Body Temperature

1) The *ENZYMES* in the cells of the human body work best at 37ºC.
2) The *HYPOTHALAMUS* senses changes and sends *NERVOUS IMPULSES* to the skin.
3) *THE SKIN* then has *three tricks* for *controlling body temperature*:

When you're TOO HOT:

1) *HAIRS* lie flat.
2) *SWEAT* is produced to cool you down.
3) The *BLOOD SUPPLY* to the skin opens up to release body heat. This is called *vasodilation*.

When you're TOO COLD:

1) *HAIRS* stand on end to keep you warm.
2) *NO SWEAT* is produced.
3) The *BLOOD SUPPLY* to the skin *CLOSES OFF*. This is called *vasoconstriction*.

Oil gland

hair erector muscle

capillary network

Sweat Gland

no sweat

hairs erect

blood supply shut off

When you're cold your body also increases metabolism to produce heat

It does this in two ways 1) By *INCREASING LIVER ACTIVITY*   2) By *SHIVERING*.
Both of these *GENERATE HEAT* inside us by *increasing metabolism* (i.e. converting more energy).

Realistically the hairs standing on end make *no difference* to humans. It's a leftover from when we had hairy bodies. However, *in your Exam* you'll dutifully mention it *to get the marks*.
These days we just put *more layers of clothes on*, to trap *more layers of air*, because *air acts as an insulator* so long as it's *trapped* and can't move around — *LEARN those details*.

So much to learn — don't let it get under your skin...

I can count about 17 important facts to learn on this page, plus a couple of suitably splendid diagrams. *Learn the headings* for each section, then *cover the page* and *scribble* out the details.

SECTION THREE — HUMAN BIOLOGY II

Kidneys

Kidneys basically act as filters to "clean the blood"

The _kidneys_ perform _three main roles_:

> 1) _Removal of urea_ from the blood.
> 2) _Adjustment of ions_ in the blood.
> 3) _Adjustment of water content_ of the blood.

1) Removal of Urea

1) _Urea_ is produced in the _liver_.
2) Proteins can't be _stored_ by the body so _excess amino acids_ are _broken down_ by the liver into fats and carbohydrates.
3) The _waste product_ is _urea_ which is passed into the blood to be _filtered out_ by the _kidneys_. Urea is also lost partly in _sweat_. Urea is _poisonous_.

2) Adjustment of Ion Content

1) _Ions_, such as sodium (Na^+) are taken into the body in _food_, and then absorbed into the blood.
2) If the food contains _too much_ of any ions then the excess ions are _removed_ by the kidneys. For example, a salty meal will contain far too much Na^+ and the kidneys will _remove the excess_ from the blood.
3) Some ions are also lost in _sweat_ (which tastes salty, you'll have noticed).
4) But the important thing to remember is that the _balance_ is always maintained by the _kidneys_.

3) Adjustment of Water Content

Water is _taken in_ to the body as _food and drink_ and is _lost_ from the body in _four ways_:

1) in _URINE_ 2) in _FAECES_ 3) in _SWEAT_ 4) in _BREATH_

Once again there's a need for the body to _constantly balance_ the water coming in against the water going out. There are two things that need saying here:

1) The amount of water in the _faeces_ is fairly _constant_.
2) The water that comes out _in the breath_ is actually _manufactured_ in the body during _respiration_: (glucose + oxygen → Carbon dioxide + _WATER_), so it _doesn't affect_ the water balance.

That means _most of the time_ (i.e. in Exam questions) the _water balance_ is between:
1) Liquids _consumed_ 2) Amount _sweated out_ 3) Amount _dumped by the kidneys_ in the _urine_.

ON A COLD DAY, if you _don't sweat_, you'll produce _more urine_ which will be _pale and dilute_.
ON A HOT DAY, you _sweat a lot_, your urine will be _dark-coloured_, _concentrated_ and _little of it_.
This is assuming that you don't _drink_ any differently. It's pretty obvious what effect drinking has.

How Much Do You Know About Kidneys? — Let's See...

Phew. There's some stuff on this page isn't there. It's definitely a perfect candidate for the exciting mini-essay method. Learn the three headings, then _cover the page_, write them down, and then _scribble a mini-essay_ for each one. Then look back and see what you missed. _Then try again._ And learn the diagram, until you can repeat that too.

SECTION THREE — HUMAN BIOLOGY II

Ultrafiltration and The Nephron

(Wasn't that a Star Trek episode?)

Nephrons are the Filtration Units in the Kidneys

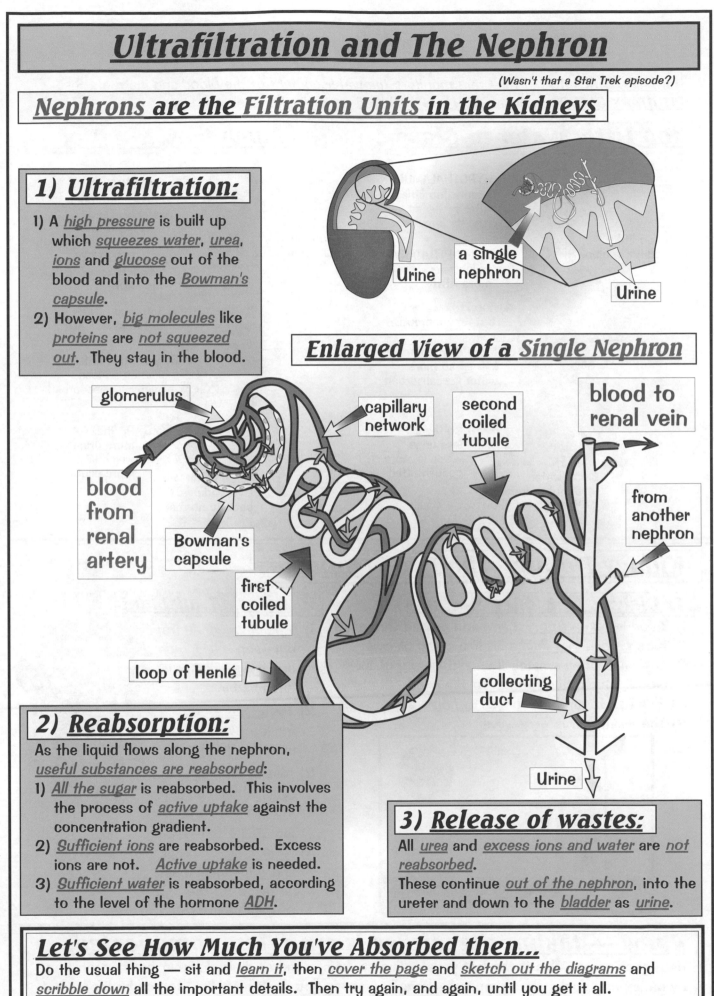

1) Ultrafiltration:

1) A _high pressure_ is built up which _squeezes water_, _urea_, _ions_ and _glucose_ out of the blood and into the _Bowman's capsule_.
2) However, _big molecules_ like _proteins_ are _not squeezed out_. They stay in the blood.

Urine

a single nephron

Urine

Enlarged View of a Single Nephron

glomerulus

capillary network

second coiled tubule

blood to renal vein

blood from renal artery

Bowman's capsule

first coiled tubule

from another nephron

loop of Henlé

collecting duct

Urine

2) Reabsorption:

As the liquid flows along the nephron, _useful substances are reabsorbed_:
1) _All the sugar_ is reabsorbed. This involves the process of _active uptake_ against the concentration gradient.
2) _Sufficient ions_ are reabsorbed. Excess ions are not. _Active uptake_ is needed.
3) _Sufficient water_ is reabsorbed, according to the level of the hormone _ADH_.

3) Release of wastes:

All _urea_ and _excess ions and water_ are _not reabsorbed_.
These continue _out of the nephron_, into the ureter and down to the _bladder_ as _urine_.

Let's See How Much You've Absorbed then...

Do the usual thing — sit and _learn it_, then _cover the page_ and _sketch out the diagrams_ and _scribble down_ all the important details. Then try again, and again, until you get it all.
I hope it's obvious that you only scribble out very rough diagrams — just to show the details.

ADH — Anti Diuretic Hormone

The **HYPOTHALAMUS** in the brain *monitors the water content of the blood* and instructs the **PITUITARY GLAND** to release **ADH** into the blood *accordingly*, as shown below:

Too Little Water in Blood

1) Too little water in blood

2) HYPOTHALAMUS detects too little water so sends nervous impulse...

3) To the PITUITARY which releases more ADH

4) Too little water but now more ADH

5) More ADH enters kidney so more water is reabsorbed

6) So there's less urine which is more concentrated

7) Blood water level not reduced

Too Much Water in Blood

1) Too much water in blood

2) HYPOTHALAMUS detects too much water so sends message to...

3) The PITUITARY which releases less ADH

4) Too much water but now less ADH

5) Less ADH enters kidney so less water is reabsorbed

6) So there's more urine which is more dilute

7) Blood water level reduced back to normal

Kidney Failure: The Two Treatments

1) Dialysis by Kidney Machine

1) Blood is *taken from an arm* and passed through a tube *bathed in a fluid* a bit like *blood plasma*.
2) *Urea* and other wastes then *diffuse out* of the blood, which then *returns to the arm*.
3) This has to be done for *12-18 hours every week*.
4) The treatment is *expensive*.

2) Kidney Transplant

1) A *healthy kidney* from a person *recently dead* or a *living relative* is "plumbed in".
2) The *blood groups* for the two people must be the *same*.
3) Ideally the *tissue types* should also be the same — if so the *success rate* is *80%*.
4) *Anti-rejection* drugs and *antibiotics* must be taken for the *rest of their life*.

Phew — taking the mickey is much less complicated...

Hey, good news. This is the last page on human beings and all their blummin' health problems. I wonder why ducks are so much healthier? Anyway you don't have time to ponder life's great imponderables such as that — you've got Exams to worry about. *Learn and scribble*... ☺

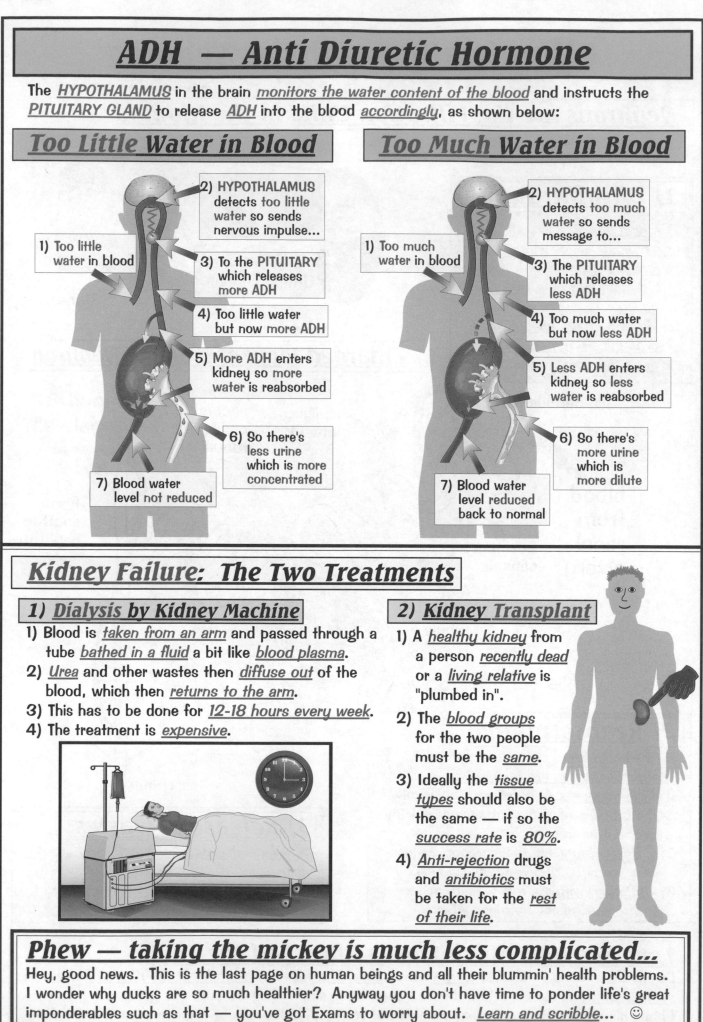

Revision Summary for Section Three

Section Three's got all sorts of grisly bits and bobs in it. And some of it can be really quite hard to understand too. But it's all worth points in the Exam, and what do points mean? Prizes! These questions are designed to test what you know. They're pretty tough I grant you, but they really are the best way of revising. Keep trying these questions any time you feel like it, and for any you can't do, look back in Section Three and learn the answer to it for next time.

1) Draw a diagram of the body and label the five places where hormones are produced.
   Give details of what each hormones does.
2) Give the proper definition of hormones. What is an endocrine gland?
3) Give four details to compare nerves with hormones.
4) Explain what happens with insulin when the blood sugar is too high and when it is too low.
5) Draw diagrams to illustrate exactly what goes on in both cases.
6) What happens in diabetes? What are the two forms of treatment? How do they compare?
7) Give brief details of the four stages in the female menstrual cycle.
8) Sketch the diagram showing the state of the uterus lining at each stage.
9) Give full details of which hormones are used: a) to promote fertility   b) in "The Pill".
10) What are the two main hormones involved in the female menstrual cycle?
11) Sketch the diagram showing the uterus lining and the levels of both over the 28 days.
12) <u>For NEAB only</u>: What are the other two hormones involved and where do they originate?
    Draw graphs showing the level of these other two hormones and explain what they both do.
13) What are the two types of microbe? How big are they compared to a human cell?
14) How exactly do bacteria make you feel ill? Sketch three common bacteria.
15) What do viruses do inside you to reproduce? Illustrate with sketches.
16) What are the five ways that microbes can enter our bodies?
17) Give details of the defences we have against these five methods of entry.
18) What is meant by your "immune system"? What is the most important part of it?
19) List the three ways that white blood cells deal with invading microbes.
20) Give full details of the process of immunisation. How does it work?
21) What are antibiotics? What will they work on and what will they not work on?
22) What are the two types of addiction to drugs?
23) List the five different types of "drug" with examples of each. List the dangers of each type.
24) Explain the dangers of drinking alcohol.   Explain why smoking is just *so cool — not.*
25) List in detail all five major health problems that result from smoking.
26) What is the proper definition for homeostasis? What are the six bodily levels involved?
27) Draw a diagram of the body showing the eight organs involved in homeostasis.
28) Say exactly what each of these organs does to help.
29) What are the three main things that the skin does for you?
30) What temperature do our bodily enzymes like?
31) Which organ detects body temperature? How does it tell the skin about it?
32) Draw diagrams showing the three things the skin does when we're a) too hot b) too cold.
33) What is the basic function of the kidneys? What *three* particular things do they deal with?
34) Explain in detail exactly what the kidney does in relation to each of these three things.
35) Sketch a kidney to show where a nephron is and then roughly draw an enlarged nephron.
36) Label the main parts of it and describe the *three main processes* and where they all happen.
37) What is ADH and where is it produced?
38) Draw diagrams to explain how ADH is involved in regulating the water content of the blood.
39) What are the two treatments for kidney failure? Give the pros and cons of both.

Variation in Plants and Animals

The word _"VARIATION"_ sounds far too fancy for its own good.
All it means is how animals or plants of the same species _look or behave slightly different from each other_. You know, a bit _taller_ or a bit _fatter_ or a bit more _scary-to-look-at_ etc.
There are _two_ causes of variation: _Genetic Variation_ and _Environmental Variation_. Read on, and learn...

1) Genetic variation

You'll know this already. _All animals_ (including humans) are bound to be _slightly different_ from each other because their _GENES_ are slightly different. Genes are the code inside all your cells which determine how your body turns out. We all end up with a slightly different set of genes.
The _exceptions_ to that rule are _identical twins_, because their genes are _exactly the same_.
But even identical twins are never _completely identical_ — and that's because of the other factor:

2) Environmental Variation _is shown up by_ Twins

If you're not sure what _"environment"_ means, think of it as _"upbringing"_ instead
— it's pretty much the same thing — how and where you were "brought up".

Nice one Pauline!

Since we know the _twins' genes_ are _identical_, any differences between them _must_
be caused by slight differences _in their environment_ throughout their lives.

Twins give us a fairly good idea of how important the _two factors_ (genes and environment) are, _compared to each other_, at least for animals — plants always show _much greater variation_ due to differences in their environment than animals do, as explained below.

Environmental _Variation_ in Plants _is much_ Greater

PLANTS are _strongly affected_ by:
1) _Temperature_   2) _Sunlight_   3) _Moisture level_   4) _Soil composition_
For example, plants may grow _twice as big_ or _twice as fast_ due to _fairly modest_ changes in environment such as the amount of _sunlight_ or _rainfall_ they're getting, or how _warm_ it is or what the _soil_ is like.

(A cat, on the other hand, born and bred in say, the North of Scotland, could be sent out to live in equatorial Africa and would show no significant changes — it would look the same, eat the same, and probably still puke up everywhere.)

To Test for the Effects of Environment on Plants

Are the differences because of their environments?

In many types of plant it's possible to produce _clones_, which are _genetically identical_ to one another, just like twins are.
  You can then expose such plants to various conditions to see how it affects them, knowing that _any differences in appearance_ are due entirely to _environment_.

  With _ordinary plants_ (which are _NOT_ clones) you have to do a bit of _experimenting_ to test how much environment is affecting them. So plants make for tricky Exam questions:

  _"If two similar plants growing next to each other
  are different sizes, what's the reason for it —
  genetic variation or differences in environment?"_

The answer is that it could be either! To find out you'd need to carry out one of these two careful _TESTS_:

1) _PLANT TWO NEW PLANTS_ of the _same species_ in the _same positions_ and see if the _same thing_ happens. If the same place gives a smaller plant _again_ you'd know the difference in size was _probably_ due to differences in the environment between the two positions.
2) Or, you could plant _THE TWO ORIGINAL PLANTS_ in _another place_ and see if they start growing more alike. If they do, it suggests that differences in _environment_ was the cause of the differences in growth.

Variation in Plants and Animals

Environmental Variation in Animals

Stubborn cats notwithstanding...
In Exams they do like questions on _the effects of environment on animals_.

Typically, they'll ask you _which features_ of a human or a pet _MIGHT be affected_ by their environment (i.e. the way they were "brought up").

In fact, _almost every single aspect_ of a human (or animal) will be affected by _upbringing_ in some way, however small, and in fact it's considerably easier to list the very few factors that _aren't_ affected by environment:

4 Animal Characteristics NOT affected at all by Environment:

1) _EYE COLOUR_
2) _HAIR COLOUR_ in most animals, (but not humans where vanity plays a big part)
3) _INHERITED DISEASES_ like haemophilia, cystic fibrosis, etc.
4) _BLOOD GROUP_

And that's about it! So _learn those four_ in case they ask you.

EVERYTHING ELSE is determined by _A MIXTURE_ of _genetic_ and _environmental_ factors:
Body weight, _height_, _skin colour_, _condition of teeth_, _academic or athletic prowess_, etc. etc.

The _tricky_ bit is working out just _how significant_ environmental factors are for all these other features.
   For example, imagine you got mixed up with another baby at the hospital and had grown up in a totally different household from your own. How different would you be now?   It's not at all easy to tell how much of your physique and (more importantly) your personality are due to genes and how much to upbringing (environment).   It's a big social issue, so it is.

Continuous and Discontinuous Variation:

CONTINUOUS VARIATION: The feature can vary over a _continuous range of values_.

Continuous variation refers to things like _height_ or _weight_ or _skin colour_, where the thing can have _any value at all_ (within reason).
   For example, the weight of a dog could be _absolutely anything_ between say 2kg and 60kg: 5.3kg, 24.2kg, 24.23kg, 24.233kg, 35.1kg etc.

DISCONTINUOUS VARIATION: The feature can only take _one of several options_.

Discontinuous variation is things like _eye colour_ or _blood group_, where there are just _a few definite options_, not a whole continuous range of possibles.
   For example, eyes can only be _blue or brown or green or hazel_. They cannot be bluey-brown or kinda-greeney-bluey, or sorta-browney-bluey-kinda-hazeley, etc.

Two other examples are _DISEASE RESISTANCE IN LEAVES_ and _LEAF AREA_.   One shows _continuous_ variation and the other shows _discontinuous_ variation. You work out which is which.

Don't let Everything get to you — just learn the facts...

There are six sections on these two pages. After you think you've learnt it all, _cover the pages_ and do a "mini-essay" on each of the six sections. Then _check back_ and see what important points you missed. The coloured ink highlights the important bits — the rest is idle creative genius.

Genetics: Too Many Fancy Words

When it comes to _big fancy words_ then _Biology_ is the subject where it's all happening.
And _genetics_ is the topic that _REALLY_ walks away with all the prizes.
It seems _hard to believe_ that so many exceptionally cumbersome, excessively complicated and virtually unintelligible words can conceivably be necessary, or indeed be particularly desirable...

Here's a summary of all the fancy words used in _genetics_ with an explanation of what they actually mean. _It really does make a big difference_ if you _learn_ these first. It's very difficult to understand _anything_ in genetics if you don't actually know what half the words mean.

DNA — is the _molecule_ which contains _genes_. It's shaped like a _double helix_ (a spiral).

Chromosomes — are those funny _X-shaped_ things that are found in the _cell nucleus_. The arms are made up of _very long coils of DNA_, so chromosomes also contain _genes_.

Chromatids — are just the _separate arms_ of the X-shaped _chromosomes_.

Centromere — is just the bit in the _middle_ of the chromosomes, where the arms _join_.

Gene — is a _section of DNA molecule_. It's also part of the _arm_ of a chromosome.

Allele — is a _gene_ too. When you have _two different versions_ of the same gene you have to call them _alleles_ instead of genes. (It _is_ more sensible than it sounds.)

Dominant — this refers to an _allele_ or _gene_. The dominant allele is the one which will _determine_ the characteristic which appears. _It dominates the recessive allele_ on the other chromosome.

Recessive — is the _allele_ which does _not_ usually affect how the organism turns out because it's _dominated_ by the dominant allele (fairly obviously).

Homozygous — is an individual with _two alleles the same_ for that particular gene, e.g. HH or hh.

Heterozygous — is an individual with _two alleles different_ for that particular gene, e.g. Hh.

Genotype — is simply a _description_ of the _genes_ you have, e.g. Mm or RR, that type of thing.

Phenotype — is the description of your _physical attributes_ due to the genes in question i.e. your _phenotype_ describes the _physical result_ (e.g. "Bald") of your _genotype_, (e.g. "bb").

Mitosis — is the process of _cell division_ where one cell splits into _two identical cells_.

Meiosis — is the other process of _cell division_ which _creates sperm or egg cells_. Meiosis only happens in the _ovaries_ or the _testes_.

Diploid — is the description of _cells_ which have _all_ 46 chromosomes i.e. _BOTH_ sets of 23.

Haploid — is the description of cells which only have _half_ the chromosomes, i.e. 23.

Gamete — is either a _sperm cell_ or an _egg cell_.
All _gametes_ are _haploid_ — they only have 23 chromosomes.

Zygote — is the delightful name given to each newly-formed human life, just after the (equally delightfully-named) _gametes_ _fuse together_ at fertilisation.

You'd think they could have come up with some slightly prettier names, as would befit this most awesome and wonderful moment, really. Your whole life, that great voyage of discovery and wonder, of emotion and reason, of conscience and consciousness, begins with that fateful and magical moment when...
..."two GAMETES fuse to form a ZYGOTE"...   _Ahh, what poetry..._

Too many fancy words, but you still gotta learn 'em...

Practise by covering up the right hand side of the page and scribbling down a description for each word. That's nice and easy. Just keep looking back and practising _till you can do them all_.

Genes, Chromosomes and DNA

If you're going to get _anywhere_ with this topic you definitely need to learn these confusing words and exactly what they mean. _You have to make sure you know_ exactly what _DNA_ is, what and where _chromosomes_ are, and what and where a _gene_ is. If you don't get that sorted out first, then anything else you read about them won't make a lot of sense to you — _will it_.

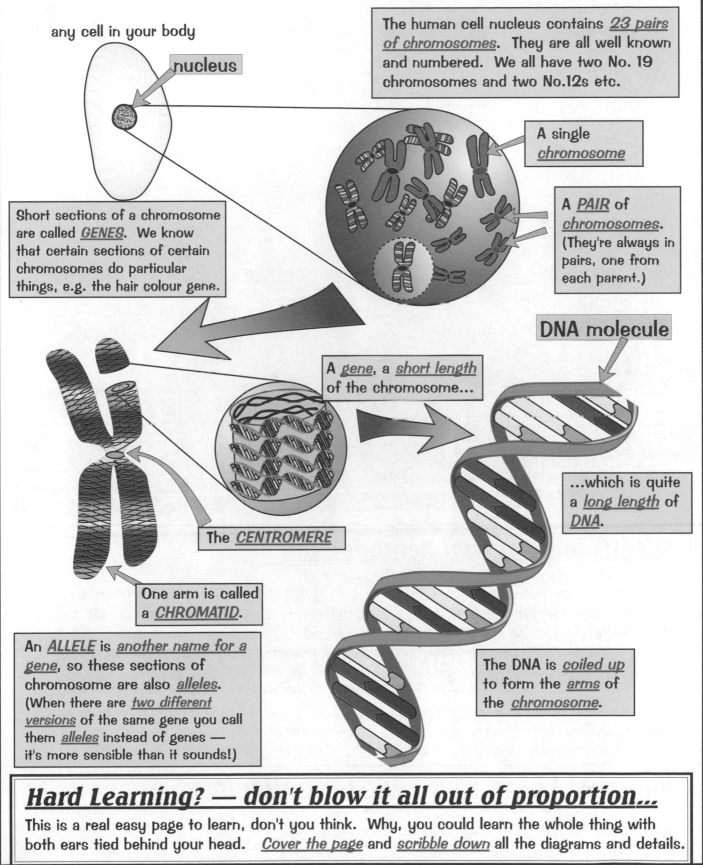

any cell in your body

nucleus

The human cell nucleus contains _23 pairs of chromosomes_. They are all well known and numbered. We all have two No. 19 chromosomes and two No.12s etc.

A single _chromosome_

A _PAIR_ of _chromosomes_. (They're always in pairs, one from each parent.)

Short sections of a chromosome are called _GENES_. We know that certain sections of certain chromosomes do particular things, e.g. the hair colour gene.

DNA molecule

A _gene_, a _short length_ of the chromosome...

...which is quite a _long length_ of _DNA_.

The _CENTROMERE_

One arm is called a _CHROMATID_.

The DNA is _coiled up_ to form the _arms_ of the _chromosome_.

An _ALLELE_ is _another name for a gene_, so these sections of chromosome are also _alleles_. (When there are _two different versions_ of the same gene you call them _alleles_ instead of genes — it's more sensible than it sounds!)

Hard Learning? — don't blow it all out of proportion...

This is a real easy page to learn, don't you think. Why, you could learn the whole thing with both ears tied behind your head. _Cover the page_ and _scribble down_ all the diagrams and details.

Ordinary Cell Division: Mitosis

"MITOSIS is when a cell reproduces itself by splitting to form two identical offspring."

The really riveting part of the whole process is how the chromosomes split inside the cell. Learn and enjoy...

DNA all spread out in *long strings*.

DNA forms into chromosomes. Remember, the *double arms* are already *duplicates* of each other.

Chromosomes line up along centre and then *the cell fibres pull them apart*.

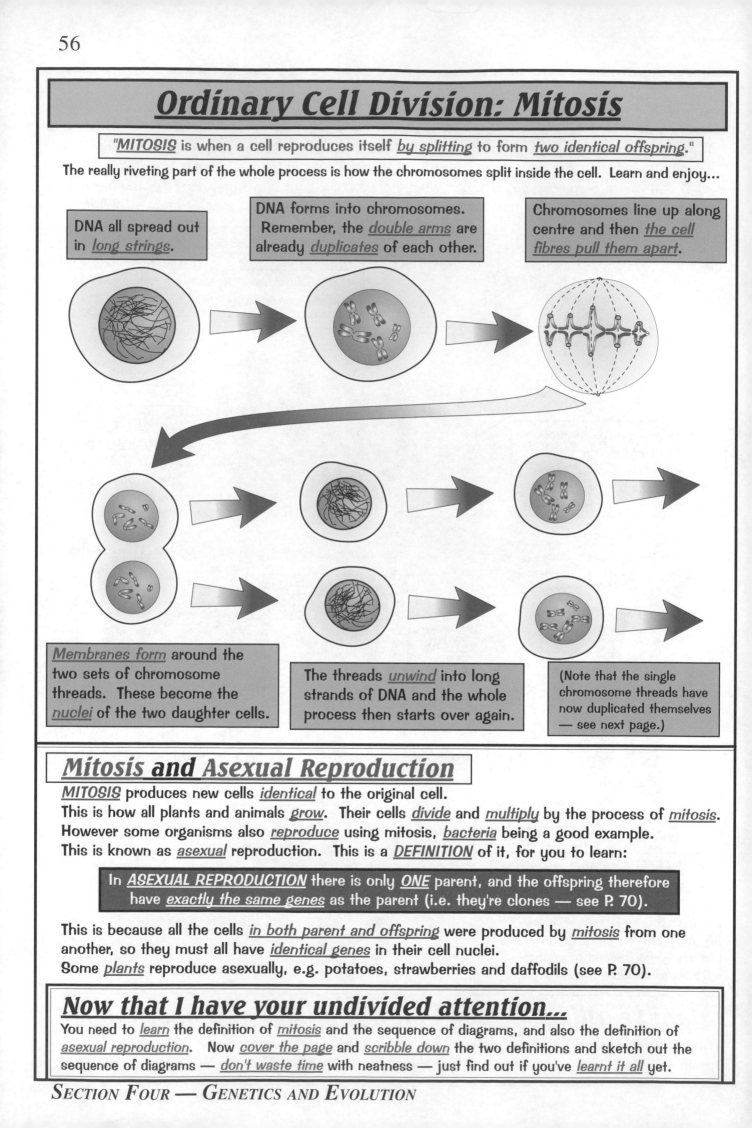

Membranes form around the two sets of chromosome threads. These become the *nuclei* of the two daughter cells.

The threads *unwind* into long strands of DNA and the whole process then starts over again.

(Note that the single chromosome threads have now duplicated themselves — see next page.)

Mitosis and Asexual Reproduction

MITOSIS produces new cells *identical* to the original cell.
This is how all plants and animals *grow*. Their cells *divide* and *multiply* by the process of *mitosis*.
However some organisms also *reproduce* using mitosis, *bacteria* being a good example.
This is known as *asexual* reproduction. This is a *DEFINITION* of it, for you to learn:

> In *ASEXUAL REPRODUCTION* there is only *ONE* parent, and the offspring therefore have *exactly the same genes* as the parent (i.e. they're clones — see P. 70).

This is because all the cells *in both parent and offspring* were produced by *mitosis* from one another, so they must all have *identical genes* in their cell nuclei.
Some *plants* reproduce asexually, e.g. potatoes, strawberries and daffodils (see P. 70).

Now that I have your undivided attention...

You need to *learn* the definition of *mitosis* and the sequence of diagrams, and also the definition of *asexual reproduction*. Now *cover the page* and *scribble down* the two definitions and sketch out the sequence of diagrams — *don't waste time* with neatness — just find out if you've *learnt it all* yet.

SECTION FOUR — GENETICS AND EVOLUTION

DNA Replication in Mitosis

Genes are Chemical Instructions

1) *A gene is a length of DNA*.
2) So DNA is a long list of *instructions* on how to put the organism together and *make it work*.
3) Each *separate gene* is a separate *chemical instruction* to a particular type of cell.
4) Cells make *proteins* by stringing *amino acids* together in a particular order.
5) There are only about *20 different amino acids*, but they make up *thousands* of different *proteins*.
6) Genes simply tell cells *in what order* to put the amino acids together.
7) That determines what *proteins* the cell produces, e.g. haemoglobin, or keratin, etc.
8) That in turn determines what *type of cell* it is, e.g. red blood cell, skin cell, etc.

DNA Replicates Itself to form Chromosomes

After mitosis, the half chromosomes *unwind themselves* into very long strands of DNA...

...which then set about *replicating* themselves:

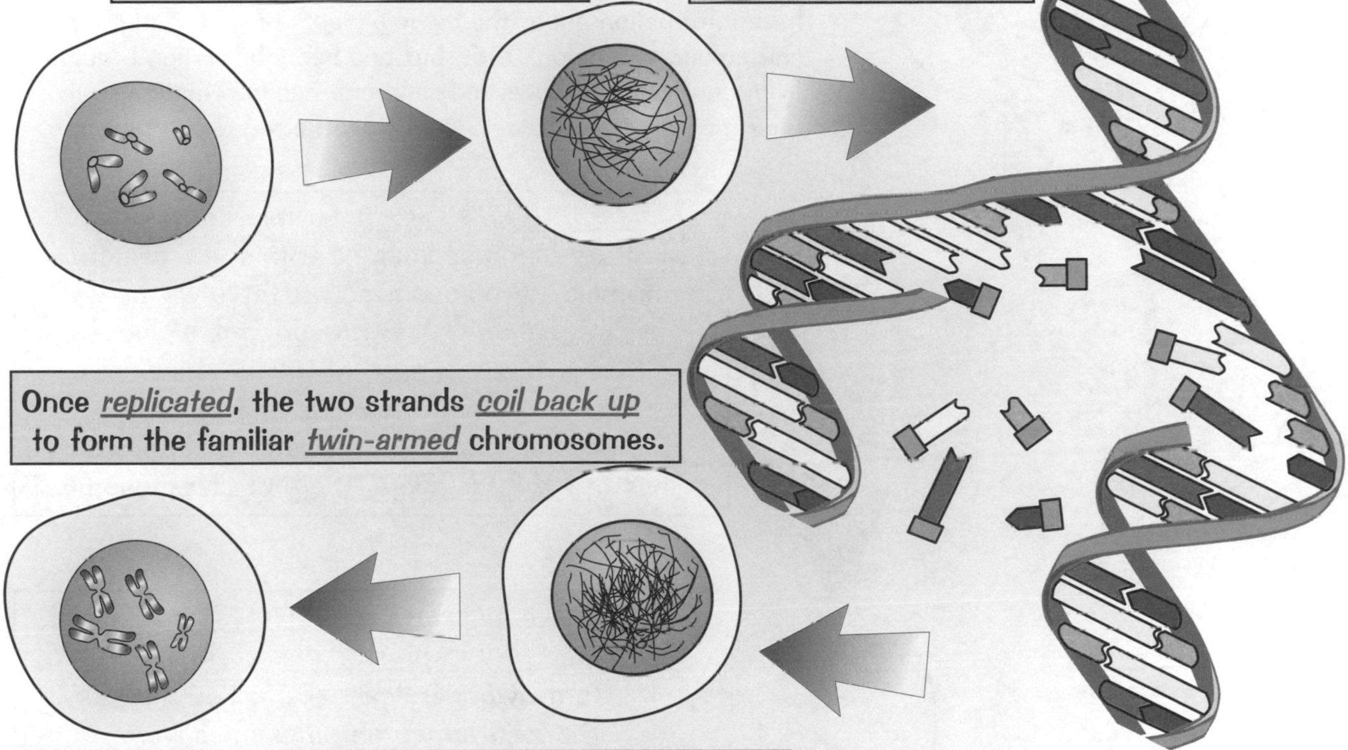

Once *replicated*, the two strands *coil back up* to form the familiar *twin-armed* chromosomes.

The arms are, of course, *copies of each other* — the *two identical strands* of DNA, joined at the centromere.

The Paired Bases make it all work

As the diagram shows, the DNA double helix is made up of just *four* different "*bases*". Make sure you realise that because these bases must **ALWAYS** pair up A-T and C-G, that as the DNA unwinds itself, new bases (floating about in the nucleus) join on *only where they fit*, and (as the diagram shows) this ensures the resulting two new DNA strands *exactly match the original*. It's all clever stuff.

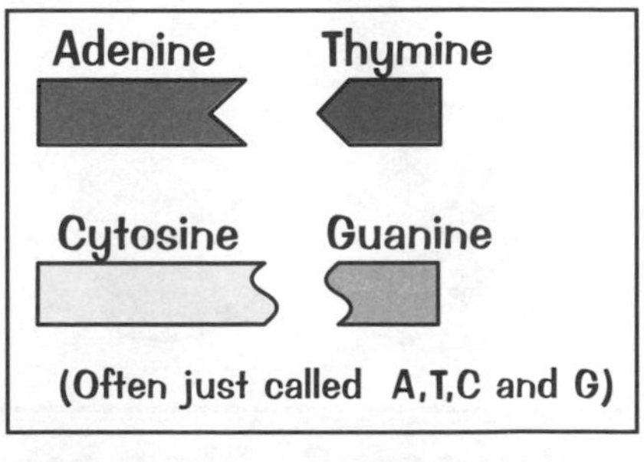

Adenine   Thymine

Cytosine   Guanine

(Often just called A,T,C and G)

Don't get all knotted up with yourself, relax and enjoy...

I have to say, I think these ace diagrams make this all very easy to learn.
You know the drill. *Cover the page* and *scribble down* the details of all three sections.

Gamete Production: Meiosis

You thought mitosis was exciting. Hah! You ain't seen nothing yet. _Meiosis_ is the other type of cell division. It only happens in the _reproductive organs_ (ovaries and testes).

> _MEIOSIS_ produces _"cells which have half the proper number of chromosomes"_.
> Such cells are also known as _"haploid gametes"_.

These cells are "genetically different" from each other because _the genes all get shuffled up_ during meiosis and each gamete only gets _half of them_, selected at random.
Confused? I'm not surprised. But fear not, my little yellow friend...
The diagrams below will make it a lot clearer — but you have to _study_ them pretty hard.

Reproductive cell in testis (or ovary).

1) Remember, there are _23 pairs_ of chromosomes at the start. That means 46 altogether, two of each type. In each _pair_, there is one you got from your _father_, and one you got from your _mother_.

They're called "_homologous pairs_" because _both_ chromosomes have information about the _same aspects_ of your body, e.g. hair colour, eye colour, etc., but one has information brought from your father (shown red) and one has information from your mother (shown blue). Note the little red y-chromosome.

2) _The PAIRS now split up_ so that some of your father's chromosomes go with some of your mother's chromosomes, but there will be _no pairs at all now_. Just _one of each_ of the 23 different types in each of the two new cells. Each cell therefore has a _mixture_ of your mother's and father's characteristics, but only has _half the full complement_ of chromosomes.

3) These cells now split _mitosis-style_, with the _chromosomes themselves splitting_ to form two identical cells, called _gametes_. The twin-armed chromosomes were already duplicates, don't forget.

And that's meiosis done.
Note the difference between the _first stage_ where the _pairs separate_ and the _second stage_ where the _chromosomes themselves split_. It's tricky!

GAMETES
i.e. sperm cells or (egg cells).

Meiosis? Not even remotely scary...

There's a few tricky words in there which don't help — especially if you just ignore them...
The only way to _learn_ this page is by constant reference to the diagram. Make sure you can sketch all the parts of it _from memory_ and _scribble notes_ to explain each stage. Even so, it's still difficult to understand it all, never mind remember it. But that's what you gotta do!

SECTION FOUR — GENETICS AND EVOLUTION

Fertilisation: The Meeting of Gametes

There are 23 Pairs of Human Chromosomes

They are well known and numbered. In every _cell nucleus_ we have _two of each type_. The diagram shows the 23 pairs of chromosomes from a human cell. _One_ chromosome in _each pair_ is inherited from _each of our parents_. Normal body cells have 46 chromosomes, in _23 homologous pairs_.

Remember, "_homologous_" means that the two chromosomes in each pair are _equivalent_ to each other. In other words, the number 19 chromosomes from both your parents _pair off together_, as do the number 17s etc. What you _don't get_ is the number 12 chromosome from one parent pairing off with, say, the number 5 chromosome from the other.

Reproductive Cells undergo Meiosis to Produce Gametes:

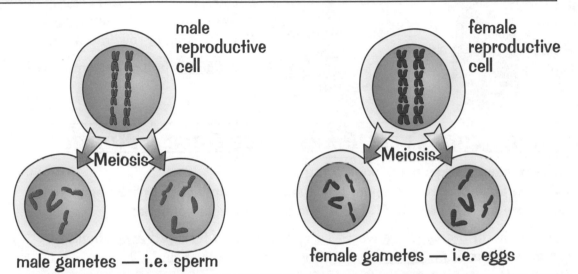

male reproductive cell

female reproductive cell

Meiosis

Meiosis

male gametes — i.e. sperm

female gametes — i.e. eggs

> The _gametes_ remember, only have _one chromosome_ to describe each bit of you, _one copy_ of each of the chromosomes numbered 1 to 23. But a _normal cell_ needs _two_ chromosomes of each type — one from _each parent_, so...

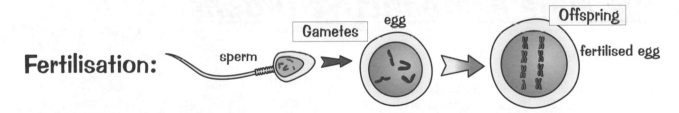

Fertilisation:

sperm

Gametes

egg

Offspring

fertilised egg

WHEN THE GAMETES MEET UP during fertilisation, the 23 single chromosomes in one gamete _will all pair off_ with their appropriate "partner chromosomes" from the other gamete to form the full 23 pairs again, No.4 with No.4, No.13 with No.13 etc. etc.

Don't forget, the two chromosomes in a pair _both contain the same basic genes_, e.g. for hair colour, etc. When single chromosomes _meet up_ at fertilisation, they _seek out_ their counterpart from the other gamete.

The resulting offspring will then receive its _outward characteristics_ as a _mixture_ from the _two_ sets of chromosomes, so it will _inherit features_ from _both parents_. Pretty cool, eh.

It should all be starting to come together now...

If you go through these last two pages you should see how the two processes, meiosis and fertilisation, are kind of opposite. Practise _sketching out_ the sequence of diagrams, with notes, for both pages till it all sinks in. Nice, innit.

Human Reproduction

You need to know the names of all the parts and what they do.

The Female Reproductive Organs

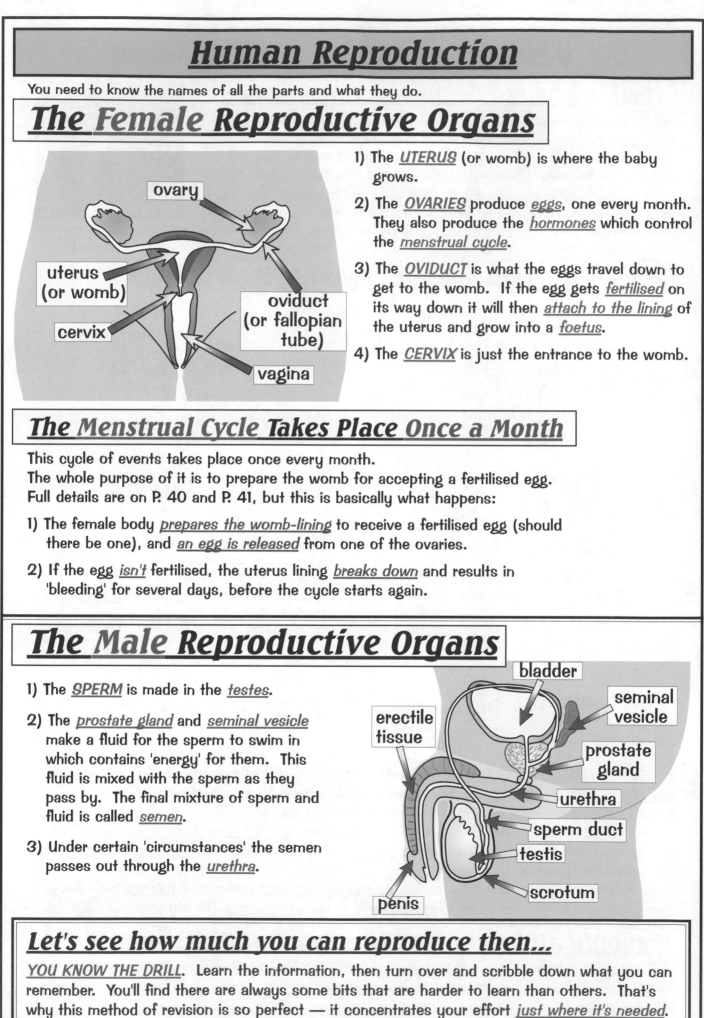

ovary

uterus (or womb)

cervix

oviduct (or fallopian tube)

vagina

1) The _UTERUS_ (or womb) is where the baby grows.

2) The _OVARIES_ produce _eggs_, one every month. They also produce the _hormones_ which control the _menstrual cycle_.

3) The _OVIDUCT_ is what the eggs travel down to get to the womb. If the egg gets _fertilised_ on its way down it will then _attach to the lining_ of the uterus and grow into a _foetus_.

4) The _CERVIX_ is just the entrance to the womb.

The Menstrual Cycle Takes Place Once a Month

This cycle of events takes place once every month.
The whole purpose of it is to prepare the womb for accepting a fertilised egg.
Full details are on P. 40 and P. 41, but this is basically what happens:

1) The female body _prepares the womb-lining_ to receive a fertilised egg (should there be one), and _an egg is released_ from one of the ovaries.

2) If the egg _isn't_ fertilised, the uterus lining _breaks down_ and results in 'bleeding' for several days, before the cycle starts again.

The Male Reproductive Organs

1) The _SPERM_ is made in the _testes_.

2) The _prostate gland_ and _seminal vesicle_ make a fluid for the sperm to swim in which contains 'energy' for them. This fluid is mixed with the sperm as they pass by. The final mixture of sperm and fluid is called _semen_.

3) Under certain 'circumstances' the semen passes out through the _urethra_.

bladder

seminal vesicle

erectile tissue

prostate gland

urethra

sperm duct

testis

scrotum

penis

Let's see how much you can reproduce then...

YOU KNOW THE DRILL. Learn the information, then turn over and scribble down what you can remember. You'll find there are always some bits that are harder to learn than others. That's why this method of revision is so perfect — it concentrates your effort _just where it's needed_.

Fertilisation and The Embryo

Fertilisation

3) Fertilisation needs to takes place _quite high up in the oviduct_, because the egg only survives for about a day.

2) _Millions_ of sperms are deposited but _only a few hundred_ reach the egg. The rest die.

Sperm are tiny, don't forget, not like those gurt "tadpoles" in the diagram

1) _Sperms are deposited_ in the vagina by an obliging male and they _swim_ up through the cervix and into the _oviducts_.

4) When the sperm reach the egg, they _cluster round it_ and eventually _one_ of them gets through the egg _membrane_.

5) The egg membrane _instantly changes_ to prevent any more sperm getting in.

6) When the _nucleus_ of the successful sperm _fuses_ with the nucleus of the egg, _fertilisation_ has taken place. A _zygote_ has then been produced.

7) If it gets fertilised, _the zygote divides_ (by mitosis) and soon becomes a veritable _ball of cells_.

8) After about _seven days_, the ball of cells reaches the uterus, where it _implants itself into the lining_. This process is called _implantation_, oddly enough. The ball of cells is now called an _EMBRYO_.

NON-IDENTICAL twins occur if _two different eggs_ get fertilised, perhaps one from each ovary. _IDENTICAL_ twins form if the new ball of cells somehow _splits in two_ at an early stage — _both halves_ then grow into full embryos.

The Embryo

The ball of cells continues to divide and multiply. When all the _organs_ have developed it's called a _foetus_. This takes about _11 weeks_.

THE PLACENTA acts as a big _exchange surface_ between the mother and baby, with _blood capillaries_ filling it from _both sides_.

FOOD AND OXYGEN diffuse across from the mother's blood and _WASTES_ are taken away by it. Unfortunately, _HARMFUL SUBSTANCES_ can also pass from the mother, such as _alcohol, bacteria, viruses and drugs_, and _carbon monoxide_ from cigarette smoking.

That's why _pregnant women_ need to be _very careful_ what they do. The growing embryo is _VERY DELICATE_ and can easily be _damaged_ by harmful things in the _mother's blood_.

The _bag_ that holds the foetus is called _THE AMNION_. It's full of _amniotic fluid_, which _protects_ the foetus from _bumps and knocks_.

ear

uterus

vagina

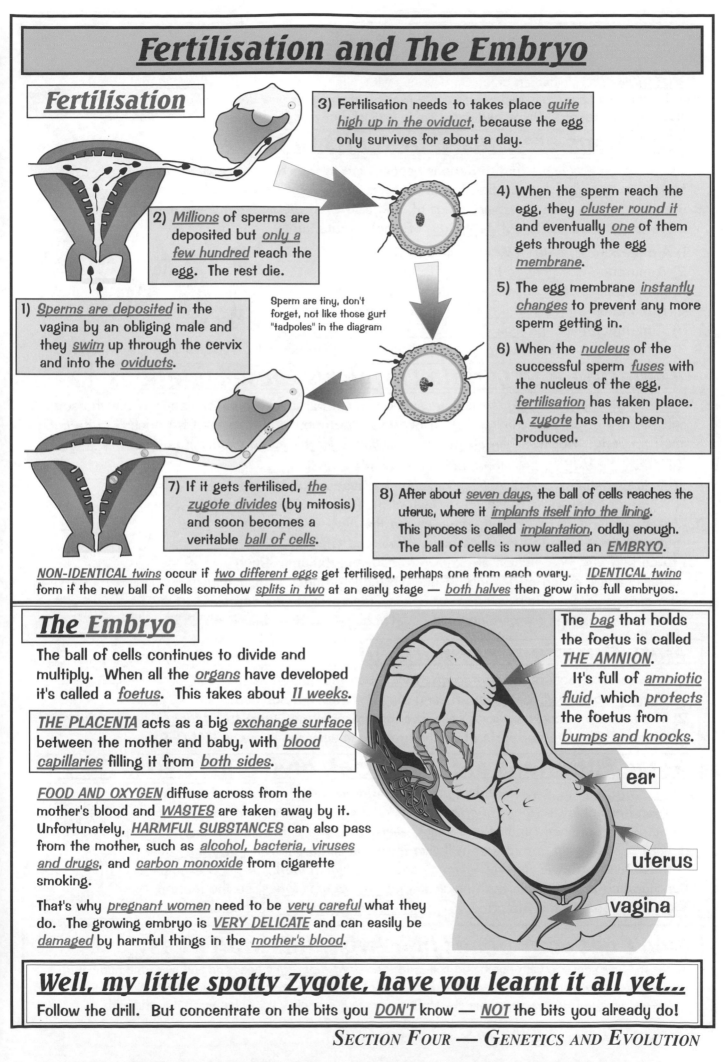

Well, my little spotty Zygote, have you learnt it all yet...

Follow the drill. But concentrate on the bits you _DON'T_ know — _NOT_ the bits you already do!

Mutations

A MUTATION occurs when an organism develops with some _strange new characteristic_ that no other member of the species has had before. For example if someone was born with blue hair it would be caused by a mutation. Some mutations are beneficial, but _most are disastrous_ (e.g. blue hair).

Mutations are Caused by Faults in the DNA

There are _several ways_ that mutations happen, but in the end they're all down to _faulty DNA_. Mutations _usually happen_ when the DNA is _replicating itself_ and something goes wrong. Because _DNA_ is what _genes_ are made of, and also what _chromosomes_ are made of, then there are all these different _definitions_ of what a mutation is:

1) A mutation is _faulty DNA_, or a change in the DNA.
2) A mutation is a _change to a gene_ or several genes.
3) A mutation is a _change_ in one or more _chromosomes_.
4) A mutation _starts in the nucleus_ of one particular cell.
5) A mutation happens _when DNA isn't copied properly_.
6) A mutation is caused by _chemical changes_ in a gene, or in the DNA, or in a chromosome.

Radiation and Certain Chemicals cause Mutations

Mutations occur 'naturally', probably caused by "natural" background radiation (from the sun, and rocks etc.) or just the laws of chance that every now and then the DNA doesn't quite copy itself properly. However _the chance of mutation is increased_ by exposing yourself:

1) to _nuclear radiation_, i.e. alpha, beta and gamma radiation. This is sometimes called _ionising radiation_ because it creates ions (charged particles) as it passes through stuff. (See the Physics Book.)
2) to _X-rays_ and _Ultra-Violet light_, which are the _highest-frequency_ parts of the _EM spectrum_ (together with _gamma rays_).
3) to certain _chemicals_ which are known to cause mutations. Such chemicals are called _mutagens_! If the mutations produce cancer then the chemicals are often called _carcinogens_. Cigarette smoke contains chemical mutagens (or carcinogens)... (I'm sayin' nowt — See P. 45).

No no! not me!

Most Mutations are Harmful

1) If a mutation occurs in _reproductive cells_, then the young may _develop abnormally_ or _die_ at an early stage of their development.
2) If a mutation occurs in body cells, the mutant cells may start to _multiply_ in an _uncontrolled_ way and _invade_ other parts of the body. This is what we know as _CANCER_.

Some Mutations are Beneficial, giving us "EVOLUTION"

1) _Blue "budgies"_ appeared suddenly as a mutation amongst yellow budgies. This is a good example of a _neutral effect_. It didn't harm its chances of survival and so it flourished (and at one stage, every grandma in Britain had one).
2) _Very occasionally_, a mutation will give the organism a survival _advantage_ over its relatives. This is _natural selection_ and _evolution_ at work. A good example is a mutation in a bacteria that makes it _resistant to antibiotics_, so the mutant gene _lives on_, in the offspring, creating a _resistant "strain"_ of bacteria.

Don't get your genes in a twist, this stuff's easy...

There are four sections with numbered points for each. _Memorise_ the headings and learn the numbered points, then _cover the page_ and _scribble down_ everything you can remember. I know it makes your head hurt, but every time you try to remember the stuff, the more it sinks in. It'll all be worth it in the end.

Girl or Boy? — X and Y Chromosomes

There are 23 matched pairs of chromosomes in every human cell. You'll notice the 23rd pair are labelled XY. They're the two chromosomes that decide whether you turn out male or female. They're called the X and Y chromosomes because they look like an X and a Y.

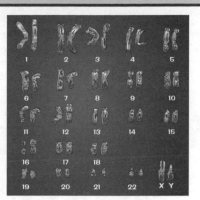

> ALL MEN have an X and a Y chromosome: XY
> The Y chromosome is DOMINANT and causes male characteristics.
>
> ALL WOMEN have two X chromosomes: XX
> The XX combination allows female characteristics to develop.

The diagram below shows the way the male XY chromosomes and female XX chromosomes split up to form the gametes (eggs or sperms), and then combine together at fertilisation.

The criss cross lines show all the possible ways the X and Y chromosomes could combine. Remember, only one of these would actually happen for any offspring.

What the diagram shows us is the RELATIVE PROBABILITY of each type of zygote (offspring) occurring.

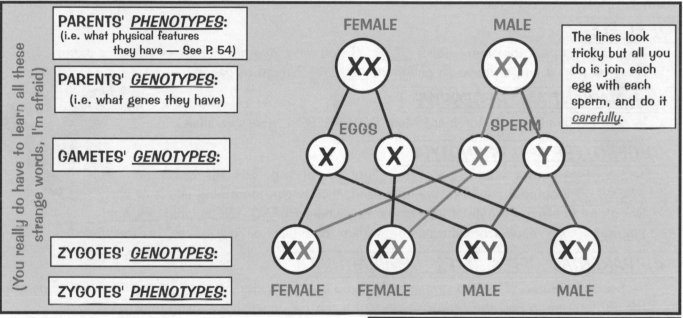

(You really do have to learn all these strange words, I'm afraid)

PARENTS' PHENOTYPES: (i.e. what physical features they have — See P. 54)

PARENTS' GENOTYPES: (i.e. what genes they have)

GAMETES' GENOTYPES:

ZYGOTES' GENOTYPES:

ZYGOTES' PHENOTYPES:

The lines look tricky but all you do is join each egg with each sperm, and do it carefully.

The other way of doing this is with a checkerboard type diagram. If you don't understand how it works, ask "Teach" to explain it. The pairs of letters in the middle show the genotypes of the possible offspring.

Both diagrams show that there'll be the same proportion of male and female offspring, because there are two XX results and two XY results.

Don't forget that this 50:50 ratio is only a probability. If you had four kids they could all be boys — yes I know, terrifying isn't it.

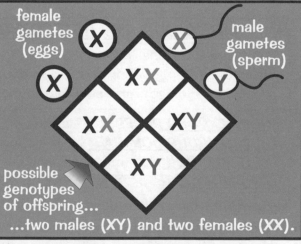

How can it take all that just to say it's a 50:50 chance...

Make sure you know all about X and Y chromosomes and who has what combination. The diagrams are real important. Practise reproducing them until you can do it effortlessly.

Monohybrid Crosses: Terminology

"Hey man, like *monohybrid crosses*, yeah right... ...so like, *what does it mean*, man?"   Just this, pal:

Breeding *two plants* or *animals*, who have *one gene different*, to see what you *get*.

It's always best done with a diagram like either of these:

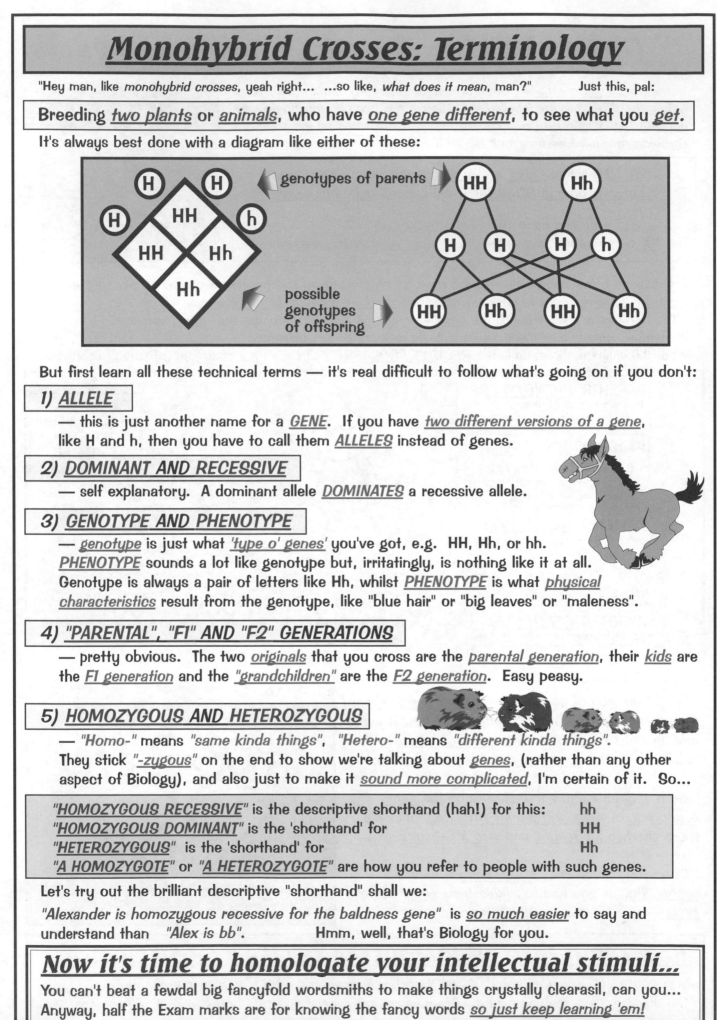

genotypes of parents

possible
genotypes
of offspring

But first learn all these technical terms — it's real difficult to follow what's going on if you don't:

1) ALLELE
— this is just another name for a *GENE*. If you have *two different versions of a gene*, like H and h, then you have to call them *ALLELES* instead of genes.

2) DOMINANT AND RECESSIVE
— self explanatory. A dominant allele *DOMINATES* a recessive allele.

3) GENOTYPE AND PHENOTYPE
— *genotype* is just what *'type o' genes'* you've got, e.g. HH, Hh, or hh. *PHENOTYPE* sounds a lot like genotype but, irritatingly, is nothing like it at all. Genotype is always a pair of letters like Hh, whilst *PHENOTYPE* is what *physical characteristics* result from the genotype, like "blue hair" or "big leaves" or "maleness".

4) "PARENTAL", "F1" AND "F2" GENERATIONS
— pretty obvious. The two *originals* that you cross are the *parental generation*, their *kids* are the *F1 generation* and the *"grandchildren"* are the *F2 generation*. Easy peasy.

5) HOMOZYGOUS AND HETEROZYGOUS
— *"Homo-"* means *"same kinda things"*, *"Hetero-"* means *"different kinda things"*. They stick *"-zygous"* on the end to show we're talking about *genes*, (rather than any other aspect of Biology), and also just to make it *sound more complicated*, I'm certain of it. So...

> *"HOMOZYGOUS RECESSIVE"* is the descriptive shorthand (hah!) for this: hh
> *"HOMOZYGOUS DOMINANT"* is the 'shorthand' for   HH
> *"HETEROZYGOUS"* is the 'shorthand' for   Hh
> *"A HOMOZYGOTE"* or *"A HETEROZYGOTE"* are how you refer to people with such genes.

Let's try out the brilliant descriptive "shorthand" shall we:

"Alexander is homozygous recessive for the baldness gene" is *so much easier* to say and understand than   *"Alex is bb"*.   Hmm, well, that's Biology for you.

Now it's time to homologate your intellectual stimuli...
You can't beat a fewdal big fancyfold wordsmiths to make things crystally clearasil, can you... Anyway, half the Exam marks are for knowing the fancy words *so just keep learning 'em!*

Monohybrid Crosses: Hamsters

Cross-breeding Hamsters

It can be all too easy to find yourself cross-breeding hamsters, some with normal hair and a mild disposition and others with wild scratty hair and a leaning towards crazy acrobatics.

Let's say that the gene which causes the crazy nature is _recessive_, so we use a _small "h"_ for it, whilst normal (boring) behaviour is due to a _dominant gene_, so we represent it with a _capital "H"_.

1) A _crazy hamster_ must have the _GENOTYPE_: hh.

2) However, a _NORMAL HAMSTER_ can have _TWO POSSIBLE GENOTYPES_: HH or Hh.

This is pretty important — it's the basic difference between dominant and recessive genes:

> To display _RECESSIVE CHARACTERISTICS_ you must have
> _BOTH ALLELES RECESSIVE_, hh, (i.e. be "homozygous recessive")
>
> But to display _DOMINANT CHARACTERISTICS_ you can be _EITHER_
> HH ("homozygous dominant") or Hh ("heterozygous").

It's only that difference which makes monohybrid crosses even _remotely_ interesting.   If hh gave crazy hamsters, HH gave normal hamsters and Hh something in between, it'd all be pretty dull.

An Almost Unbearably Exciting Example

Let's take a _thoroughbred crazy hamster_, genotype hh, with a _thoroughbred normal hamster_, genotype HH, and cross breed them. You must learn this whole diagram thoroughly, till you can do it all yourself:

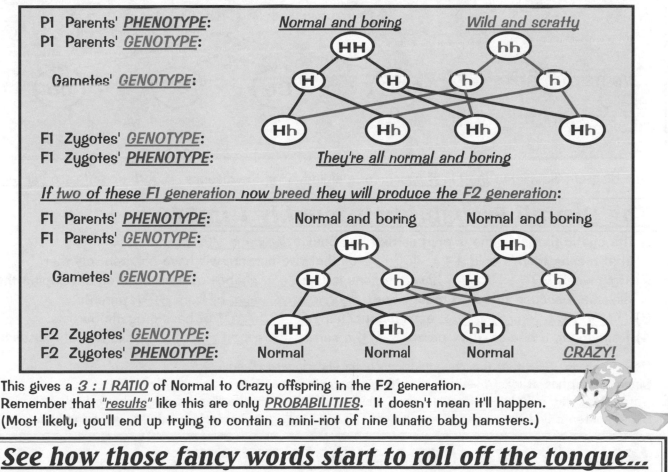

P1 Parents' _PHENOTYPE_:	_Normal and boring_ _Wild and scratty_
P1 Parents' _GENOTYPE_:	HH hh
Gametes' _GENOTYPE_:	H H h h
F1 Zygotes' _GENOTYPE_:	Hh Hh Hh Hh
F1 Zygotes' _PHENOTYPE_:	_They're all normal and boring_

If two of these F1 generation now breed they will produce the F2 generation:

F1 Parents' _PHENOTYPE_:	Normal and boring Normal and boring
F1 Parents' _GENOTYPE_:	Hh Hh
Gametes' _GENOTYPE_:	H h H h
F2 Zygotes' _GENOTYPE_:	HH Hh hH hh
F2 Zygotes' _PHENOTYPE_:	Normal Normal Normal _CRAZY!_

This gives a _3 : 1 RATIO_ of Normal to Crazy offspring in the F2 generation.
Remember that _"results"_ like this are only _PROBABILITIES_. It doesn't mean it'll happen.
(Most likely, you'll end up trying to contain a mini-riot of nine lunatic baby hamsters.)

See how those fancy words start to roll off the tongue...

The diagram and all its fancy words need to be second nature to you. So practise writing it out _from memory_ until you get it all right. Because when you can do one — _you can do 'em all_.

Cystic Fibrosis

The Symptoms

1) _CYSTIC FIBROSIS_ is a _GENETIC DISEASE_ which affects about _1 in 1600 people_ in the UK.
2) It's _caused by a defective gene_ on one of the chromosomes which the person inherits from their parents.   There's still _no cure_ or effective treatment for this condition.
3) The result of the _defective gene_ is that the body produces a lot of thick sticky mucus in the lungs, which has to be removed by _massage_.
4) Excess mucus also occurs in the _pancreas_, causing _digestive problems_.
5) Much more seriously though, _THE BLOCKAGE OF THE AIR PASSAGES_ in the lungs causes a lot of _CHEST INFECTIONS_.
6) _Physiotherapy and antibiotics_ clear them up but slowly the sufferer becomes more and more ill.

Cystic Fibrosis is Caused by a Recessive Gene (Allele)

The _genetics_ behind cystic fibrosis is actually very straightforward.
The gene which causes cystic fibrosis is a _recessive gene_, c, carried by about _1 person in 20_.
The usual genetic inheritance diagram illustrates what goes on:

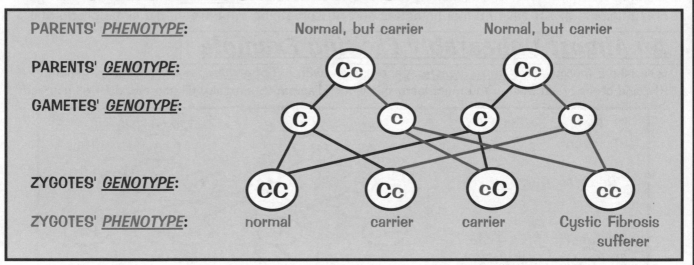

PARENTS' _PHENOTYPE_: Normal, but carrier   Normal, but carrier

PARENTS' _GENOTYPE_: Cc   Cc

GAMETES' _GENOTYPE_: C   c   C   c

ZYGOTES' _GENOTYPE_: CC   Cc   cC   cc

ZYGOTES' _PHENOTYPE_: normal   carrier   carrier   Cystic Fibrosis sufferer

This diagram illustrates _the 1 in 4 chance_ of a child having the disease, _if both parents are carriers_.

The Overall Probability is roughly 1 in 1600

1) The cystic fibrosis gene is only carried by about _1 person in 20_.
   That means there's only a _1 in 400 chance_ that two carriers will have children together.
2) Only when _BOTH PARENTS_ have the gene is there _any chance_ of their children developing the disease, because the child must inherit _the recessive allele_, c, from _BOTH_ parents.
3) _If both parents are carriers_, each baby has a _1 IN 4 CHANCE_ of having cystic fibrosis.
4) Remember, if one or other parent is _NOT_ a carrier, there's _no risk_ of any child with the disease.

It was only in _1989_ that the _gene_ causing cystic fibrosis was _discovered_.
Since then it has at least been possible to _test_ parents to see if they are _carriers_.
Before that, the only indication was when a child suffering from the disease _was actually born_.
If _both_ parents find they _are_ carriers, there's still a _difficult decision_ to be made about having kids.

Learn the facts then see what you know...

The symptoms and probabilities should be relatively easy to learn. The genetic diagram is also quite straightforward, once you get familiar with it. _Learn the whole page_, then _cover it up_ and _scribble it out_.

Haemophilia

The Symptoms

1) The main symptom of haemophilia is that _BLOOD DOES NOT CLOT_ properly.
2) This means that even _small cuts_ and _tooth extractions_ can be _LETHAL_, due to blood loss.
3) Small knocks can cause _internal bleeding_ and _big bruises_, and _joints_ may also _bleed_.
4) These days, however, the condition can be _treated quite successfully_ by regular injections of the _clotting factor_, _FACTOR 8_.

Haemophilia — the Sex-linked Gene

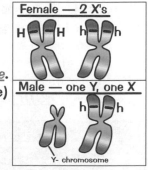

Female — 2 X's

Male — one Y, one X

Y- chromosome

1) A _SEX-LINKED_ condition is one which is _only present in either males or females_.
2) _HAEMOPHILIA_ is only present in _MALES_.
3) Sex-linked conditions occur when there's a _defective allele_ on the _X-chromosome_.
4) A man inherits _only one X-chromosome_ (and a "Y"— that's what makes him male)
5) However, the Y-chromosome is _SHORTER_ than the X-chromosome and so has quite a few genes _MISSING_.
6) Any _RECESSIVE_ genes on the man's single X-chromosome will therefore _express themselves_ if their equivalent is _missing_ on his Y-chromosome (see diagram).
7) In haemophilia, _the man gets the recessive allele h_ on the _X-chromosome_ that he inherits _from his mother_ (rather than the allele H which would instruct cells to produce the clotting factor). The allele h is _recessive_, but because the shorter Y-chromosome (which he gets from his dad) has _no equivalent allele_, H or h, _the recessive h allele is able to express itself_ (as haemophilia).

The Genetics of a Sex-Linked Disease

For the _BLOOD CLOTTING ALLELE_, (H or h) there are _FIVE POSSIBLE COMBINATIONS_:

1) NORMAL MALE: X^HY
2) HAEMOPHILIAC MALE: X^hY
3) NORMAL FEMALE: X^HX^H
4) CARRIER FEMALE: X^HX^h
5) zygote doesn't develop — X^hX^h

NOTE THAT:
1) You can't have a _male_ carrier without him _having the disease_.

2) There are _no female sufferers_, because any X^hX^h offspring _simply don't develop_.

To write down the genotypes for _any sex-linked genes_, you _MUST INDICATE THE X AND Y_ (chromosomes) as well as the H and h (alleles), as shown above, and below.   _DON'T FORGET_!

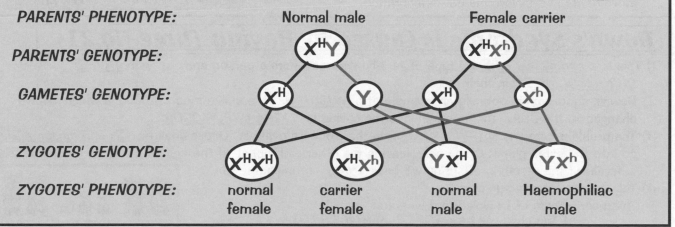

PARENTS' PHENOTYPE:	Normal male		Female carrier
PARENTS' GENOTYPE:	X^HY		X^HX^h
GAMETES' GENOTYPE:	X^H Y		X^H X^h
ZYGOTES' GENOTYPE:	X^HX^H X^HX^h		YX^H YX^h
ZYGOTES' PHENOTYPE:	normal female carrier female		normal male Haemophiliac male

Note: _If_ the mother is a _carrier_, there's a _1 in 4 chance_ of each of her children having the disease.

Learn the facts then see what you know...

There are various ways they could test your knowledge of haemophilia in the Exam. The numbered facts are relatively easy marks. For trickier questions you'll need to be able to easily reproduce any of the stuff in the coloured boxes. So practise _learning and understanding_ it till you can.

Other Genetic Diseases

Sickle Cell Anaemia — Caused by a Recessive Allele

1) This disease causes the _RED BLOOD CELLS_ to be shaped like _SICKLES_ instead of the normal round shape.
2) They then get _stuck_ in the capillaries which _deprives body cells of oxygen_.
3) It's an unpleasant, painful disease and sufferers die at an early age.
4) Yet even though sufferers _die before they can reproduce_, the occurrence of sickle cell anaemia _doesn't always die out_ as you'd expect it to, especially not in _Africa_.
5) This is because _carriers_ of the recessive allele which causes it _ARE MORE IMMUNE TO MALARIA_. Hence, being a carrier _increases_ their chance of survival in some parts of the world, even though some of their offspring are going to die young from sickle cell anaemia.
6) The genetics are _identical_ to _Cystic Fibrosis_ because both diseases are caused by a _recessive allele_. Hence if _BOTH_ parents are carriers there's a _1 in 4 chance_ each child will develop it:

PARENTS PHENOTYPE:	Normal, but carrier	Normal, but carrier
PARENTS GENOTYPE:	Ns	Ns
GAMETES' GENOTYPE:	N s	N s
ZYGOTES' GENOTYPE:	NN Ns	sN ss
ZYGOTES' PHENOTYPE:	normal carrier	carrier Sickle cell sufferer

Huntington's Chorea is caused by a Dominant Allele

1) _UNLIKE_ Cystic Fibrosis and Sickle Cell Anaemia, this disease is caused by a _DOMINANT allele_.
2) This results in a _50% CHANCE_ of each child inheriting the disease _IF JUST ONE PARENT_ is a carrier. _THESE ARE SERIOUSLY GRIM ODDS_.
3) The _"carrier"_ parent will of course be a _sufferer_ too since the allele is dominant, but the _symptoms do not appear until after the age of 40_, by which time the allele has been passed on to _children_ and even _grandchildren_. Hence the disease persists.
4) The disease isn't nice, resulting in shaking, erratic body movements and severe mental deterioration.

Carrier/sufferer — normal
Hn   nn
H   n   n   n
Hn   Hn   nn   nn
Sufferer Sufferer normal normal

Down's Syndrome is Caused by Having Three No.21s

1) This is a _completely different_ type of genetic disease where a person ends up with _THREE CHROMOSOME 21s_ in their cells.
2) Down's syndrome is actually an example of a _MUTATION_. It is unlike most mutations which involve changes to the DNA. This one just involves having an _EXTRA CHROMOSOME_.
3) The problem happens _DURING MEIOSIS_ in the woman's ovaries. Occasionally _BOTH chromosome 21s_ go into the same gamete (egg cell), leaving the other with none. If the egg with two chromosome 21s is fertilised the resulting offspring will have _THREE_ chromosome 21s.
4) This causes Down's syndrome.
   The main effects of Down's Syndrome are:
   a) The child will have _LOWER MENTAL ABILITY_.
   b) They are also generally _more susceptible to certain diseases_.
   c) They tend to _DIE QUITE YOUNG_, around the age of thirty.

20   21   22

Learn the facts then see what you know...

These diseases are all mentioned in the _syllabuses_ and questions on them are _very likely_. You need to _learn_ all this very basic information on all three. _Cover the page_ and _scribble_ it all down.

Selective Breeding

Selective Breeding is Very Simple

SELECTIVE BREEDING is also called _artificial selection_, because humans artificially select the plants or animals that are going to breed and flourish, according to what _WE_ want from them. This is the basic process involved in selective breeding:

1) From your existing stock select the ones which have the _BEST CHARACTERISTICS_.
2) _Breed them_ with each other.
3) Select the _best_ of the _OFFSPRING_, and combine them with the best that you already have and _breed again_.
4) Continue this process over _SEVERAL GENERATIONS_ to _develop_ the _desired traits_.

Selective Breeding is Very Useful

Artificial Selection like this is used in _most areas of modern farming_, to great benefit:
1) Selectively breeding _BEEF CATTLE_ to get the _best beef_ (taste, texture, appearance, etc.).
2) Selectively breeding _MILKING COWS_ to increase _milk yield_ and _resistance to disease_.
3) Selectively breeding _CHICKENS_ to improve _egg size_ and _number of eggs_ per hen.
4) Selectively breeding _WHEAT_ to produce new varieties with better _yields_ and better _disease-resistance_ too.
5) Selectively breeding _FLOWERS_ to produce _bigger_ and _better_ and _more colourful ones_.

The Main Drawback is a Reduction in the Gene Pool

1) Selective breeding reduces the _number of alleles_ in a population because the farmer keeps breeding from the "best" animals or plants — the same ones all the time.
2) This can cause problems if a _new disease appears_, as there may be no plants with different alleles (genes) _resistant_ to it, and therefore nothing to selectively breed a new strain from.

Selective Breeding in Pedigree Dogs Causes Bad Health

Most of the above _doesn't apply_ to selective breeding in _pedigree dogs_ where _physical appearance_ is the _only thing_ that seems to matter — purely for winning dog shows. Many pedigree dogs (in fact _most_ pedigree dogs) have quite bad _health problems_ because of this artificial selection.

Mongrels (random cross-breeds) on the other hand, are usually much healthier, fitter dogs because they're not so interbred. They're very often much nicer natured and they can be real pretty too. The word "mongrel" does them no justice at all. If you want a really great dog, my advice is go to the dog rescue place and get a crazy cross-breed and just love him.

Don't sit there brooding over it, just learn the info...

Selective breeding is a very simple topic. In the Exam they'll likely give you half a page explaining how a farmer in Sussex did this or that with his crops or cows, and then they'll suddenly ask: "_What is meant by selective breeding_". That's when you just write down the four points at the top of the page. Then they'll ask you to "_Suggest other ways that selective breeding might be used by farmers in Sussex to improve their yield_". That's when you just list some of the six examples that you've learnt.
They do like padding the questions out, don't they! In Olden Times (the 1970s) they would just have said: "_Explain what selective breeding is and give four examples of where it is used. — 8 Marks_" (!)

Cloned Plants

Learn this definition of clones: | CLONES are GENETICALLY IDENTICAL ORGANISMS

Clones occur naturally in both plants and animals. Identical twins are clones of each other.
These days clones are very much a part of the high-tech farming industry.

Many Plants Reproduce Asexually — all by themselves

This means they produce exact genetic copies of themselves without
involving another plant. Here are three common ones:

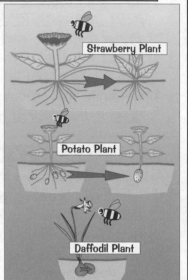

Strawberry Plant

Potato Plant

Daffodil Plant

1) STRAWBERRY PLANTS producing runners.
2) New POTATO PLANTS growing from tubers of old plant.
3) Bulbs such as DAFFODILS growing new bulbs off the side of them.

These Plants Must Also Reproduce Sexually

All of these plants also reproduce SEXUALLY — i.e. they attract insects to get
cross-pollinated and hence produce genetically DIFFERENT offspring.
Strawberry, daffodil and potato plants produce flowers for this very purpose.

This is very important because cloning has the very serious drawback that
there's no genetic variation amongst a population of clones so a change in
environment, especially a new disease, could wipe the whole lot out. If a
particular disease kills one of the clones, it will kill all the rest too.
Not too good for the survival of the species, it has to be said.

Micropropagation and Tissue Culture

Gardeners are familiar with taking cuttings from good parent plants, and then planting them to produce
copies (clones) of the parent plant — they then make ideal Christmas gifts, it would seem. These days,
this basic technique has been given the full high-tech treatment by commercial plant breeders:

The Essentials of high-tech Micropropagation:

1) A STEM is cut into many short sections, each with a new BUD on.
2) These sections are STERILISED and put into individual containers with a
   "GROWTH MEDIUM" which also contains ROOTING HORMONES.
3) Each stem section grows into a TINY PLANTLET with roots.
4) They are developed in a damp atmosphere until big enough, then
   "toughened up" in a greenhouse.

TISSUE CULTURE | is where, instead of starting with at least a stem and bud,
they just put A FEW PLANT CELLS in a growth medium with hormones and
it just grows into A NEW PLANT. Just like that! Phew.

Growth
medium
with rooting
hormones

ADVANTAGES OF TISSUE CULTURE:

1) Very FAST — can produce thousands of plantlets in a few weeks.
2) Very little SPACE needed. 3) CAN GROW ALL YEAR — no problem with weather or seasons.
4) New plants are DISEASE-FREE. 5) NEW PLANTS can be DEVELOPED (very quickly) by
   splicing new genes into plantlets and seeing how they turn out.

DISADVANTAGES OF TISSUE CULTURE:

Only the usual drawback with clones — a reduced "gene pool" leading to vulnerability to new diseases.

Stop Cloning Around (and just learn it...

I hope you realise that they could easily test your knowledge of any sentence on this page. I only put
in stuff you need to know, you know. Practise scribbling out all the facts on this page, mini-essay style.

Cloned Cows and Genetic Engineering

Embryo Transplants in Cows

Normally, farmers only breed from their _BEST_ cows and bulls. However, such traditional methods would only allow the _prize cow_ to produce _one new offspring each year_. These days the whole process has been transformed using _EMBRYO TRANSPLANTS_:

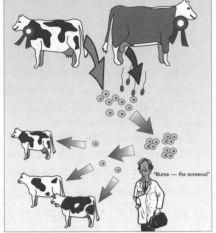

1) _SPERM_ are taken from the prize bull.
2) They're checked for _genetic defects_ and which _SEX_ they are.
3) They can also be _FROZEN_ and used at a later date.
4) Selected prize cows are given _HORMONES_ to make them produce _LOTS OF EGGS_.
5) The cows are then _ARTIFICIALLY INSEMINATED_.
6) _THE EMBRYOS_ are taken from the prize cows and checked for sex and genetic defects.
7) The embryos are developed and _SPLIT_ (to form _CLONES_) before any cells become specialised.
8) These embryos are _IMPLANTED_ into other cows, where they grow. They can also be _FROZEN_ and used at a later date.

"Nurse — the screens!"

ADVANTAGES OF EMBRYO TRANSPLANTS:
    a) _Hundreds_ of "ideal" offspring can be produced _every year_ from the best bull and cow.
    b) The original prize cow can keep producing _prize eggs all year round_.
DISADVANTAGES:
    Only the _usual drawback with clones_ — a reduced _"gene pool"_ leading to _vulnerability to new diseases_.

Genetic Engineering is Ace — hopefully

This is a new science with exciting possibilities, but _dangers_ too. The basic idea is to _move sections of DNA_ (genes) from one organism to another so that it produces _useful biological products_. We presently use bacteria to produce _human insulin_ for diabetes sufferers and also to produce _human growth hormone_ for children who aren't growing properly.

Genetic Engineering involves these Important Stages:

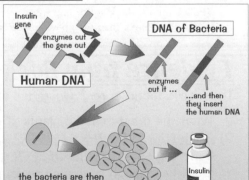

Insulin gene

enzymes cut the gene out

DNA of Bacteria

Human DNA

enzymes cut it ...

...and then they insert the human DNA

the bacteria are then grown like mad...

Insulin

1) The useful gene is _"CUT"_ from the DNA of say a human.
2) This is done using _ENZYMES_. Particular enzymes will cut out particular bits of DNA.
3) _ENZYMES_ are then used to _cut the DNA_ of a _bacterium_ and the human gene is then inserted.
4) Again this _"SPLICING"_ of a new gene is controlled by certain _specific enzymes_.
5) The bacterium is now _CULTIVATED_ and soon there are _millions_ of similar bacteria all producing, say human insulin.
6) This can be done on an _INDUSTRIAL SCALE_ and the useful product can be _separated out_.

Hence we've turned nasty old bacteria into _a useful biological factory_. Phew, that's modern science for you.

The same approach can also be used to _transfer useful genes into ANIMAL EMBRYOS_. Sheep for example can be developed which produce useful substances (i.e. drugs) _in their milk!_ This is a very easy way to produce drugs...

Hmmph... Kids these days, they're all the same...

Once again, they could ask you about any of the details on this page. The only way to be sure you know it: _cover the page_ and write _mini-essays_ on both topics. Then see what you missed, and _try again_...

Fossils

FOSSILS are the _"remains"_ of plants and animals which lived _millions of years ago_.

There are Three ways that Fossils can be Formed:

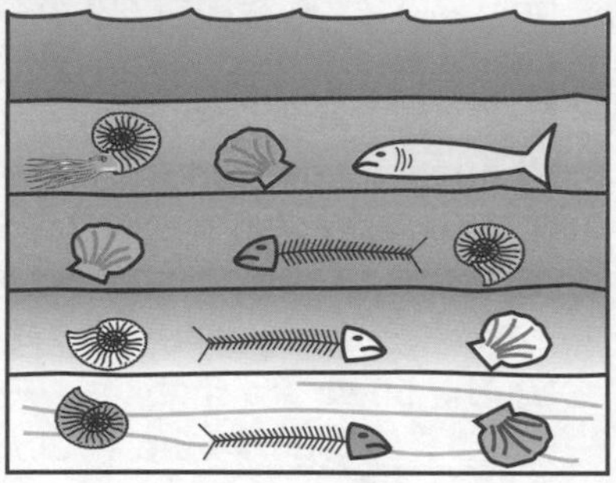

1) FROM THE _HARD PARTS_ OF ANIMALS (Most fossils happen this way.)

Things like _bones_, _teeth_, _shells_, etc., which _don't decay_ easily, can last a long time when _buried_. They're eventually _replaced by minerals_ as they decay, forming a _rock-like substance_ shaped like the original hard part. The surrounding sediments also turn to rock, but the fossil stays _distinct_ inside the rock, and eventually someone _digs it up_.

2) FROM THE _SOFTER PARTS_ OF ANIMALS OR PLANTS — _PETRIFICATION_

Sometimes fossils are formed from the _softer parts_ which somehow haven't decayed. The soft material gradually becomes _"petrified"_ (turns to stone) as it slowly decays and is _replaced by minerals_. This is _rare_, since there are _very few occasions_ when decay occurs so _slowly_.

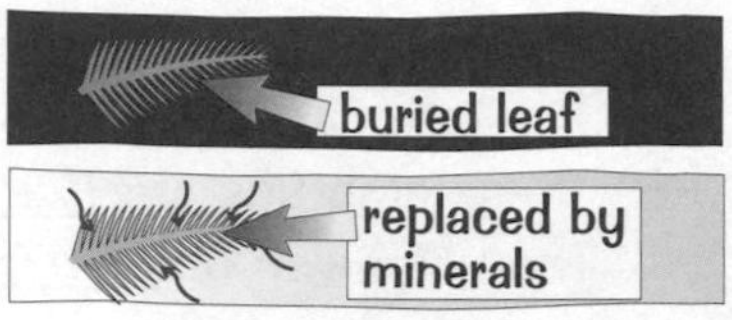

buried leaf

replaced by minerals

3) IN PLACES WHERE _NO DECAY_ HAPPENS

The _whole original plant or animal_ may survive for _thousands of years_:

a) _AMBER_ — no _OXYGEN_ or _MOISTURE_ for the _decay microbes_.

INSECTS are often found _fully preserved_ in amber, which is a clear yellow "stone" made of _FOSSILISED RESIN_ that ran out of an ancient tree hundreds of millions of years ago, engulfing the insect.

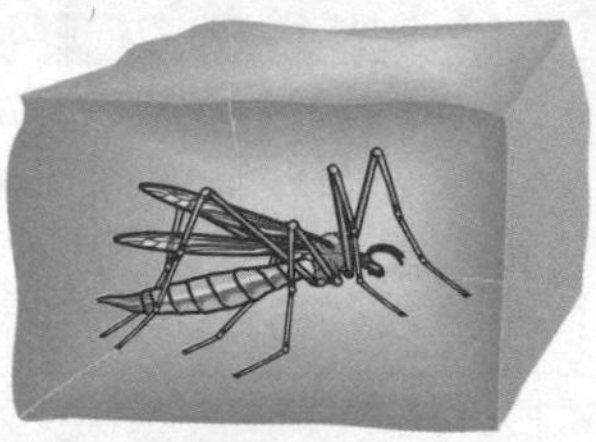

b) _GLACIERS_ — too _COLD_ for the _decay microbes_ to work.

A _HAIRY MAMMOTH_ was found fully preserved in a glacier somewhere several years ago
(at least that's what I heard, though I never saw any pictures of it so maybe it was a hoax, I'm not really sure, but anyway in principle one could turn up any time...)

c) _WATERLOGGED BOGS_ — too _ACIDIC_ for _decay microbes_.

A _10,000 year old man_ was found in a bog a few years ago. He was dead, and a bit squashed but otherwise quite well preserved, although it was clear he had been murdered.
(Police are not looking for any witnesses and have asked anyone _else_ who thinks they may have important information to just keep away.)

Evidence from Rock and Soil Strata

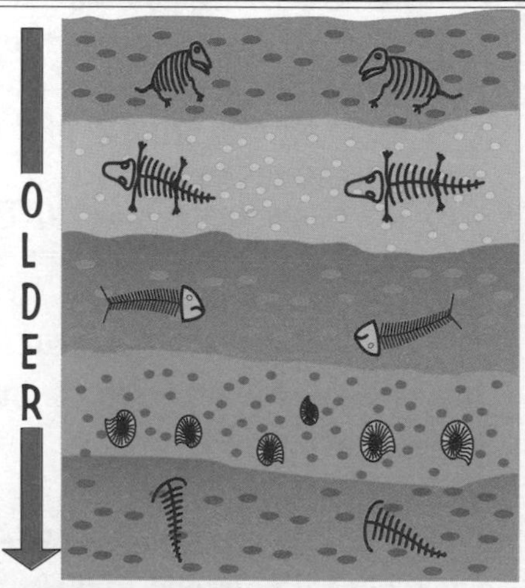

The fossils found in _rock layers_ tell us _TWO THINGS_:

1) What the creatures and plants _LOOKED LIKE_.
2) _HOW LONG AGO THEY EXISTED_, by the type of rock they're in. Generally speaking, the _DEEPER_ you find the fossil, the _OLDER_ it will be, though of course rocks get pushed upwards and eroded, so very old rocks can become exposed.

Fossils are usually _dated_ by geologists who _ALREADY KNOW THE AGE OF THE ROCK_. The Grand Canyon in Arizona is about _1 mile deep_. It was formed by a river slowly cutting down through layers of rock. The rocks at the bottom are about _1,000,000,000 years old_, and the fossil record in the sides is pretty cool.

O L D E R

Don't get bogged down in all this information...

Make sure you're fully aware of the _three_ different types of _fossil_ and how they're _formed_. Also make sure you learn all the details about what information rocks provide. Many people read stuff and then think they know it. It's only if you _cover it up_ that you find out what you _really_ know.

SECTION FOUR — GENETICS AND EVOLUTION

Evolution

The Theory of Evolution is Cool

1) This suggests that all the animals and plants on Earth gradually _"evolved"_ over _millions of years_, rather than just suddenly popping into existence. Makes sense.

2) Life on Earth began as _simple organisms living in water_ and gradually everything else evolved from there. And it only took about _3,000,000,000 years_.

Fossils Provide Evidence for it

1) _Fossils_ provide lots of _evidence_ for evolution.

2) They show how today's species have _changed and developed_ over _millions of years_.

3) There are quite a few "_missing links_" though because the fossil record is _incomplete_.

4) This is because _very very few_ dead plants or animals actually turn into fossils.

5) Most just _decay away_ completely.

The Evolution of The Horse is Ace

1) One set of fossils which _is_ pretty good though is that showing _the evolution of the horse_.

2) This developed from quite a small creature about the size of a _dog_ and the fossils show how the _middle toe_ slowly became bigger and bigger and eventually evolved into the familiar _hoof_ of today's horse.

3) It took about _60 million years_ though.

4) This is _pretty strong evidence_ in support of _evolution_ because it really shows evolution happening!

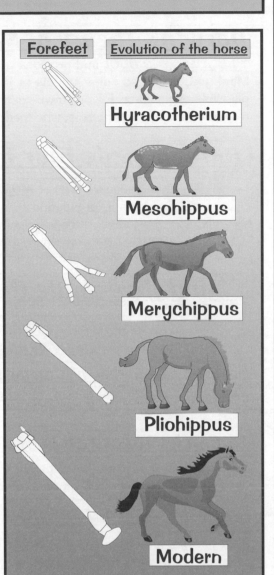

Forefeet | Evolution of the horse

Hyracotherium

Mesohippus

Merychippus

Pliohippus

Modern

Extinction is Pretty Bad News

The _dinosaurs_ and _hairy mammoths_ became _EXTINCT_ and it's only _FOSSILS_ that tell us they ever existed at all, (notwithstanding the odd questionable glacier story).

There are _THREE WAYS_ a species can become _EXTINCT_:
1) The _ENVIRONMENT CHANGES_ too quickly.
2) A new _PREDATOR_ or _DISEASE_ kills them all.
3) They can't _COMPETE_ with another (new) species for _FOOD_.

As the environment _slowly changes_, it will gradually favour certain new characteristics amongst the members of the species and over many generations those features will _proliferate_. In this way, the species _constantly adapts_ to its changing environment. But if the environment changes _too fast_ the whole species may be _wiped out_, i.e. _extinction_...

Stop horsing around and just learn the facts...

Another stupefyingly easy page to learn. Use the _mini-essay_ method. Just make sure you _learn every fact_, that's all. Dinosaurs never did proper revision and look what happened to them. (Mind you they did last about 200 million years, which is about 199.9 million more than we have, so far...)

Natural Selection

Darwin's Theory of Natural Selection is Ace

THIS THEORY IS COOL and provides _a comprehensive explanation for all life on Earth_.
Mind you, it caused some trouble at the time, because for the first time ever, there was a highly plausible explanation for our own existence, without the need for a "Creator". This was _bad news_ for the religious authorities of the time, who tried to ridicule old Charlie's ideas. But, as they say, _"THE TRUTH WILL OUT"_.

Darwin made Four Important Observations...

1) All organisms produce _MORE OFFSPRING_ than could possibly survive.
2) But in fact, population numbers tend to remain _FAIRLY CONSTANT_ over long periods of time.
3) Organisms in a species show _WIDE VARIATION_ due to different genes.
4) _SOME_ of the variations are _INHERITED AND PASSED ON_ to the next generation.

...and then made these Two Deductions:

1) Since most offspring don't survive, all organisms must have to _STRUGGLE FOR SURVIVAL_.
2) The ones who _SURVIVE AND REPRODUCE_ will _PASS ON THEIR GENES_.

This is the famous _"SURVIVAL OF THE FITTEST"_ statement. Organisms with slightly less survival-value will probably perish first, leaving the _strongest and fittest_ to _pass on their genes_ to the next generation.

Lamarck's Theory on Evolution — talk about sticking your neck out

Darwin's theory of evolution is pretty obviously right. There was another theory which they seem to want you to know about by a chap called _LAMARCK_. His theory was that:

Animals _EVOLVE FEATURES_ according to how much they _USE THEM_.

So _giraffes_, ever _stretching_ to higher branches and _straining their necks_, passed on this fact to their offspring, who were then _born_ with _slightly longer necks_. The theory isn't great and seems to be _comprehensively disproved_ by experiments on _mice_ who had their _tails cut off_ for generation after generation and still grew tails _just as long_ even though their forefathers _never made any use_ of theirs.

Mutations play a big part in Natural Selection...

...by creating a _new feature_ with a _high survival value_. Once upon a time maybe all rabbits had _short ears_ and managed OK. Then one day out popped a mutant with _BIG EARS_ who was always the first to dive for cover. Pretty soon he's got a whole family of them with _BIG EARS_, all diving for cover before the other rabbits, and before you know it there's only _BIG-EARED_ rabbits left because the rest just didn't hear trouble coming quick enough.

(Eat your heart out, Rudyard Kipling)

All Wild Creatures live in a very Harsh World indeed...

...which causes many to _DIE YOUNG_, due to _PREDATORS_, _DISEASE_ and _COMPETITION_.
But remember, _this is an important element_ in the process of _NATURAL SELECTION_.
There has to be _a LARGE SURPLUS of offspring_ for nature to _select the fittest_ from.
    Life for any _farm animal_ is a veritable dream compared to the "_eat or be eaten_" savage reality of the 'natural' world. Most wild animals are eventually either _eaten alive_ or else they _starve to death_. Think about it — _they've all gotta go somehow_. Give them a nice cosy civilised farm any day, I say...

"Natural Selection" — sounds like Vegan Chocolates...

This page is split into five sections. _Memorise_ the headings, then _cover the page_ and _scribble down_ all you can about each section. Keep trying until you can _remember_ all the important points.

Revision Summary for Section Four

Gee, all that business about genes and chromosomes and the like — it's all pretty serious stuff, don't you think? It takes a real effort to get your head round it all. There's too many big fancy words, for one thing. But there you go — life's tough and you've just gotta face up to it.
Use these questions to find out what you know — and what you don't. Then look back and learn the bits you didn't know. Then try the questions again, and again...

1) What are the two types of variation? Describe their relative importance for plants and animals.
2) List four features of animals which aren't affected at all by environment, and four which are.
3) What is meant by continuous and discontinuous variation? Give two examples of each.
4) On P. 54 there are 18 fancy words to do with genetics. List them all — with explanations.
5) Draw a set of diagrams showing the relationship between: cell, nucleus, chromosomes, genes, DNA.
6) Give a definition of mitosis. Draw a set of diagrams showing what happens in mitosis.
7) What is asexual reproduction? Give a proper definition for it. How does it involve mitosis?
8) Genes are chemical instructions. Give details of exactly what instructions they give.
9) Draw a set of diagrams to show how single armed chromosomes become double armed ones.
10) What are the names of the four "bases"? How do they make DNA replication work so well?
11) Where does meiosis take place? What kind of cells does meiosis produce?
12) Draw out the sequence of diagrams showing what happens during meiosis.
13) How many pairs of chromosomes are there in a normal human cell nucleus?
14) What happens to the chromosome numbers during meiosis and then during fertilisation?
15) Draw a diagram of the main parts of the female and male reproductive systems.
16) Describe what each bit does. What is the female menstrual cycle for?
17) Draw a sequence of diagrams showing how sperm reach the egg and fertilise it.
18) Also describe what happens to the fertilised egg as it travels on down to the uterus.
19) What is implantation? What is the difference between a zygote, an embryo and a foetus?
20) Sketch a foetus in the womb. Show the amnion and placenta and explain what they do.
21) Give four definitions of what a mutation is. List the four main causes of mutations.
22) Give an example of harmful, neutral and beneficial mutations.
23) What are X and Y chromosomes to do with? Who has what combination?
24) Draw a genetic inheritance diagram to show how these genes are passed on.
25) What is meant by monohybrid crosses?
26) Give three examples of the wonderful genetics descriptive shorthand.
27) Starting with parental genotypes HH and hh, draw a full genetic inheritance diagram to show the eventual genotypes and phenotypes of the F1 and F2 generations (of hamsters).
28) List the symptoms and treatment of cystic fibrosis. What causes this disease?
29) Draw a genetics diagram to show the probability of a child being a sufferer.
30) How does the overall probability work out to 1 in 1600? What advance was made in 1989?
31) Give the symptoms and treatment of haemophilia.
32) What is meant by a sex-linked condition? Draw the X and Y chromosomes to illustrate.
33) Show the five possible combination of genes in haemophilia and draw the genetic diagram.
34) Give the cause and symptoms of sickle cell anaemia. Why does it not die out?
35) Explain the grim odds for Huntington's Chorea. Explain why Down's Syndrome is a mutation.
36) Describe the basic procedure in selective breeding (of cows). Give five other examples.
37) What is the main drawback of selective breeding in a) farming b) pedigree dogs?
38) Write down all you know on cloned plants and micropropagation.
39) Give a good account of embryo transplants, and a good account of genetic engineering.
40) Describe fully the three ways that fossils can form. Give examples of each type.
41) Explain how fossils found in rocks support the theory of evolution. Refer to the horse.
42) What were Darwin's four observations and two deductions? Is it a cosy life for wild animals?
43) Describe Lamarck's theory of evolution and give evidence against it.

Population Sizes

POPULATION SIZE just means how many of _one type of plant or animal_ there is in a given ecosystem, and more importantly, _WHY ONLY THAT MANY_, why not more? The answer is that there are always _LIMITING FACTORS_, such as _too little food_ or _too many other animals_ eating the food as well, or _too many animals eating them_, etc... This can all start to get out of hand and sound really complicated. But it's _really very simple_, and you must keep telling yourself that!

Limits on Animal and Plant Populations

Approach 1 — the size of the population of any animal or plant is due to _SIX FACTORS_:

1) The _TOTAL AMOUNT OF FOOD_ or nutrients available.
2) The amount of _COMPETITION_ there is (from other species) for the same food or nutrients.
3) The _AMOUNT OF LIGHT AVAILABLE_ (this applies only to plants really).
4) The _NUMBER OF PREDATORS_ (or grazers) who may eat the animal (or plant) in question.
5) _DISEASE_.
6) _MIGRATION_, i.e. some of the animals moving away to another place.

Approach 2 — the size of the population of any animal or plant is due to _THREE FACTORS_:

1) _ADAPTATION_ — how well the animal has become _adapted to its environment_.
2) _COMPETITION_ — how well the animal _competes with other species_ for the same food.
3) _PREDATION_ — how well the animal _avoids being eaten_.

In the Exam they could ask you about it from either viewpoint. Although these lists seem kind of hard to relate to, what they're saying is surely just common sense ...

In other words... organisms will thrive best if:

1) _THERE'S PLENTY OF THE GOOD THINGS IN LIFE_: food, water, space, shelter, light, etc.
2) _THEY'RE BETTER THAN THE COMPETITION AT GETTING IT_ (better _adapted_).
3) _THEY DON'T GET EATEN_.
4) _THEY DON'T GET ILL_.

That's pretty much the long and the short of it, wouldn't you say?   So learn those four things. Every species is different, of course, but those _FOUR_ basic principles will always apply. In Exam questions _YOU_ have to apply them to any new situation to work out what'll happen.

Populations of Prey and Predators go in Cycles

In a community containing prey and predators (as most of them do of course):

1) The _POPULATION_ of any species is usually _limited_ by the amount of _FOOD_ available.
2) If the population of the _PREY_ increases, then so will the population of the _PREDATORS_.
3) However as the population of predators _INCREASES_, the number of prey will _DECREASE_.

    i.e. _More grass_ means _more rabbits_.
       More rabbits means _more foxes_.
       But more foxes means _less rabbits_.
       Eventually less rabbits will mean _less foxes again_.
       This _up and down pattern_ continues...

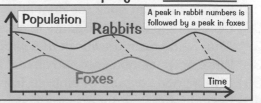

A peak in rabbit numbers is followed by a peak in foxes

Revision stress — don't let it eat you up...

It's a strange topic is population sizes. In a way it seems like common sense, but it all seems to get so messy. Anyway, _learn all the points on this page_ and you'll be OK with it, I'd think.

Adapt and Survive

If you *learn the features* that make these animals well adapted, you'll be able to apply them to any other similar animal they might give you in the Exam. Chances are you'll get a *camel* or a *polar bear* anyway.

The Polar Bear — Designed for Arctic Conditions

The *Polar bear* has all these features: (which *many other arctic creatures* have too, so think on...)

1) *Large size* and *compact shape* (i.e. rounded), including dinky little ears, to keep the *surface area* to a *minimum* (compared to the body weight) — this all *reduces heat loss*.
2) A *thick layer of blubber* for *insulation* and also to survive hard times when *food is scarce*.
3) *Thick hairy coat* for keeping the body heat in.
4) *Greasy fur* which *sheds water* after swimming to *prevent cooling* due to evaporation.
5) *White fur* to match the surroundings for *camouflage*.
6) *Strong swimmer* to catch food in the water and *strong runner* to run down prey on land.
7) *Big feet* to *spread the weight* on snow and ice.

The Camel — Designed for Desert Conditions

The *camel* has all these features: (most of which are shared by *other desert creatures*...)

1) It can *store* a lot of *water* without problem. It can drink up to *20 gallons* at once.
2) It *loses very little water*. There's *little urine* and *very little sweating*.
3) It can tolerate *big changes* in its own *body temperature* to remove need for sweating.
4) *Large feet* to *spread load* on soft sand.
5) All *fat* is stored in the *hump*, there is *no layer of body fat*. This helps it to *lose* body heat.
6) *Large surface area*. The shape of a camel is anything but compact, which gives it more surface area to *lose body heat* to its surroundings.
7) Its *sandy colour* gives good *camouflage*.

The Lion — a perfect Predator

1) *Strong*, *agile* and *fast*.
2) *Strong jaws* and *sharp teeth* for killing prey.
3) Good *stereo vision* with both eyes *facing forwards*.
4) *Camouflaged body* for stalking prey.
5) The right sort of *teeth* for *chewing meat*.

The Rabbit — a perfect Prey

1) *Fast* and *agile* for escaping capture.
2) Eyes on sides for *all-round vision*.
3) *Big ears* for good hearing.
4) *Brown colour* for *camouflage*.
5) *White tail* to alert pals.

Creature features — learn and survive...

It's worth learning all these survival features well enough to be able to write them down *from memory*. There's a whole world full of animals and plants, all with different survival features, but explaining them eventually becomes kinda "common sense", because the same principles tend to apply to them all.

SECTION FIVE — ENVIRONMENT

Atmospheric Pollution

The Three Main Sources of Atmospheric Pollution are...

1) Burning fossil fuels

1) _Fossil fuels_ are _coal_, _oil_ and _natural gas_.
2) The main culprits who burn these are _cars_ and _power stations_.
3) They release mostly _carbon dioxide_, which is causing the _greenhouse effect_.
4) But they also release _sulphur dioxide_ and _oxides of nitrogen_, which are causing _acid rain_.

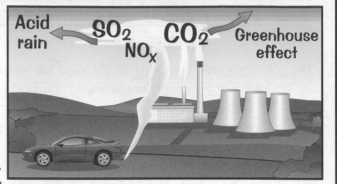

Acid rain ← SO_2 NO_X CO_2 → Greenhouse effect

2) CFC's (Chloro-fluoro-carbons)

1) These are used in _aerosols_, _fridges_, _air-conditioning units_, and _polystyrene foam_.
2) They are causing a _hole_ in the _ozone layer_.
3) This allows _harmful UV rays_ to reach the Earth's surface.

3) Lead used in Petrol

1) "Old-fashioned" _leaded_ (_4 star_) petrol contains _lead_ which pollutes the air.
2) The lead is _breathed in_ and causes damage to the _nervous system_.

People are usually OK at remembering _the three sources_ of pollution in the atmosphere, but when it comes to _sorting out their effects_, it's a whole different ball game. You have to make _a real effort_ to _learn_ exactly _where_ each type of pollution comes from and _exactly what the effect_ of each pollutant is. For example, sulphur dioxide does not affect the Greenhouse Effect one squidget, and neither do CFCs. There are dozens of ways to get them all mixed up, _but there are no marks for being a clot_.

CFCs Cause The Hole in The Ozone Layer

1) _Ozone_ is molecules made of _three oxygen atoms_, O_3.
2) There is a _layer_ of ozone _high up_ in the atmosphere.
3) Ozone _absorbs_ harmful UV rays from the sun.
4) _CFC gases_ react with ozone molecules and _break them up_.
5) This _thinning_ of the ozone layer allows _harmful UV rays_ to reach the _surface_ of the Earth.

Ozone Layer

CFCs rising up

Harmful UV rays from the Sun

Ozone Layer

6) This is making it _dangerous_ to go out in the _sun_ in many parts of the world due to the _increased risk_ of _skin cancer_ from the harmful UV rays.
7) CFCs are being replaced by _other gases_ now, but the harmful effects of the CFCs _already released_ may continue for _centuries_.

Revision and Pollution — the two bugbears of modern life...

You must make a _real effort_ to sort out the different types of air pollution. Notice for example that cars give out _three_ different things which cause _three_ different problems. _Learn it good_.

The Greenhouse Effect

Carbon Dioxide and Methane Trap Heat from the Sun

1) The _temperature_ of the Earth is a _balance_ between the heat it gets _from the sun_ and the heat it _radiates back out into space_.

Labels in diagram: Light energy from the Sun — Layer of CO_2 and Methane — Heat radiation reflected back to Earth

2) The _atmosphere_ acts like an _insulating layer_ and keeps some of the heat _in_.
3) This is exactly what happens in a _greenhouse_ or a _conservatory_.
   The sun shines _into it_ and the glass _keeps the heat in_ so it just gets _hotter and hotter_.
4) There are _several different gases_ in the atmosphere which are very good at _keeping the heat in_. They are called "_greenhouse gases_", oddly enough. The _main ones_ that we worry about are _methane_ and _carbon dioxide_, because the levels of these are _rising quite sharply_.
5) The _Greenhouse Effect_ is causing the Earth to _warm up_ very slowly.

The Greenhouse Effect may cause Flooding and Drought ....(!)

1) _Changes_ in _weather patterns_ and _climate_ could cause problems of _drought_ or _flooding_.
2) The _melting_ of the _polar ice-caps_ would _raise sea-levels_ and could cause _flooding_ to many _low-lying coastal parts_ of the world including _many major cities_.

Modern Industrial Life is Causing the Greenhouse Effect

1) The _level of CO_2_ in the atmosphere used to be _nicely balanced_ between the CO_2 _released by respiration_ (of animals and plants) and the CO_2 _absorbed by photosynthesis_.
2) However, mankind has been burning _massive amounts_ of _fossil fuels_ in the last _two hundred years_ or so.
3) We have also been _cutting down trees_ all over the world to make space for living and farming. This is called _deforestation_.
4) The level of CO_2 in the atmosphere has _gone up_ by about _20%_, and will _continue to rise_ ever more steeply as long as we keep _burning fossil fuels_ — just look at that graph — eek!

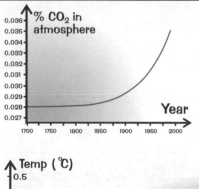

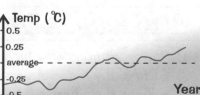

Methane is Also a Problem

1) _Methane gas_ is also contributing to the _Greenhouse Effect_.
2) It's produced _naturally_ from various sources, such as _natural marshland_.
3) However, the two sources of methane which are _on the increase_ are:
   a) _Rice growing_
   b) _Cattle rearing_ — it's the cows "pumping" that's the problem, believe it or not.

Learn the facts first — then start building your ark...

I bet you never realised there were so many drivelly details on the Greenhouse Effect.
Well there _are_ and I'm afraid they could all come up in your Exam, so you just gotta learn them.
Use the good old _mini-essay_ method for each section, and _scribble down what you know_...

Acid Rain

Burning Fossil Fuels Causes Acid Rain

1) When *fossil fuels* are *burned* they release mostly *carbon dioxide* which is causing the *Greenhouse Effect*.   They *also* release *two* other *harmful gases*:
      a) *SULPHUR DIOXIDE*   b) various *NITROGEN OXIDES*
2) When these *mix with clouds* they form *acids*. This then falls as *acid rain*.
3) *Cars* and *power stations* are the *main causes* of acid rain.

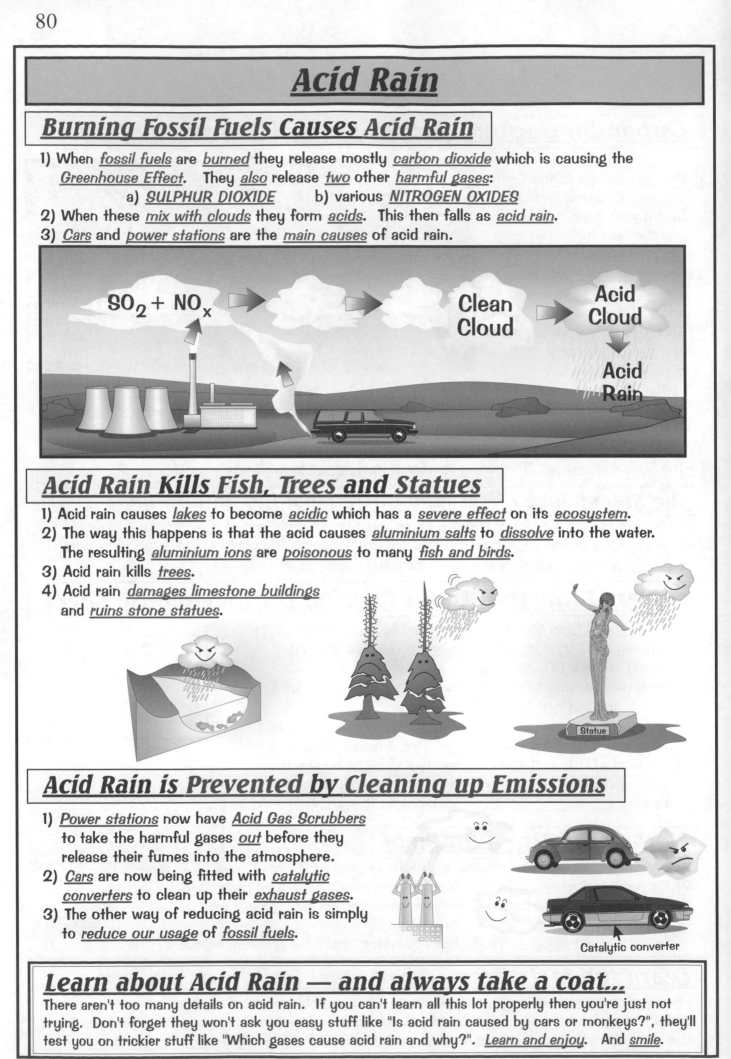

$SO_2 + NO_x$

Clean Cloud

Acid Cloud

Acid Rain

Acid Rain Kills Fish, Trees and Statues

1) Acid rain causes *lakes* to become *acidic* which has a *severe effect* on its *ecosystem*.
2) The way this happens is that the acid causes *aluminium salts* to *dissolve* into the water. The resulting *aluminium ions* are *poisonous* to many *fish and birds*.
3) Acid rain kills *trees*.
4) Acid rain *damages limestone buildings* and *ruins stone statues*.

Statue

Acid Rain is Prevented by Cleaning up Emissions

1) *Power stations* now have *Acid Gas Scrubbers* to take the harmful gases *out* before they release their fumes into the atmosphere.
2) *Cars* are now being fitted with *catalytic converters* to clean up their *exhaust gases*.
3) The other way of reducing acid rain is simply to *reduce our usage* of *fossil fuels*.

Catalytic converter

Learn about Acid Rain — and always take a coat...

There aren't too many details on acid rain. If you can't learn all this lot properly then you're just not trying. Don't forget they won't ask you easy stuff like "Is acid rain caused by cars or monkeys?", they'll test you on trickier stuff like "Which gases cause acid rain and why?". *Learn and enjoy*.   And *smile*.

There's Too Many People

The World Population is Rising Out of Control due to Modern Medicine and Agriculture

1) The _population of the world_ is currently _rising out of control_ as the graph shows.
2) This is mostly due to _modern medicine_ which has stopped widespread death from _disease_.
3) It's also due to _modern farming methods_ which can now provide the _food_ needed for so many hungry mouths.

[Graph: World population / billion people (y-axis, 0 to 6) vs Year (x-axis, 1000 to 2000). Label: "eek!" and "Introduction of modern medicine and farming"]

There's one born every minute — and it's too many

1) The _death rate_ is now _much lower_ than the _birth rate_ in many under-developed countries. In other words there are _lots more babies born_ than people _dying_.

2) This means the _population_ must be _rising_.
3) In many _poor countries_ it's rising _very quickly_.
4) This creates _big problems_ for those countries trying to _cope_ with all those _extra_ people.
5) Even providing _basic health care_ and _education_ (about _contraception!_) is difficult, never mind finding them _places to live_, and _food to eat_. If a population grows _too fast_, it creates _very severe difficulties_.
6) Unfortunately, it's a _very difficult_ problem to solve — and it's getting _rapidly worse_.

More People Means More Environmental Damage

1) As these poorer countries gradually become more _industrialised_ and with _rapidly growing populations_, the demands on the _limited resources_ of the Earth are increasing sharply.

2) _Pollution levels_ are also _increasing_, as they burn _wood_ and _fossil fuels_ to power their _growing economies_, and use up their _mineral reserves_ to create material comforts, (just like we do, don't forget).

3) And _deforestation_ is as rampant as ever, to make _more room_ for people and their _farming_. The great _rainforests_ of the world are being _destroyed_ at an _alarming rate_ by the countries which contain them, in order to make room for _cattle rearing_ and their _out-of-control_ human _populations_.

4) It _can't carry on_ like this forever. Something real bad will happen if it isn't sorted out pretty soon. That's for sure.

Learn the facts first — then you can build your rocket...

It's real scary innit — the way that graph of world population seems to be pointing nearly vertically upwards... tricky. Anyway, you just worry about your Exams instead, and make sure you learn all the grim facts. Three sections — _mini-essays_ for each, _till you know it all_.

Problems Caused By Farming

Farming Produces a Lot of Food, Which is Great, but...

1) _Farming is important_ to us because it allows us to produce _a lot of food_ from _less and less land_.
2) These days it has become quite a _high-tech_ industry. Food production is _big business_.
3) The great advantage of this is a _huge variety_ of _top quality_ foods, _all year round_, at _cheap prices_.
4) This is a far cry from Britain _50 years ago_ when food had to be _rationed_ by the government because _there simply wasn't enough_ for everyone. That's hard to imagine today... but try...

...Intensive Farming Can Destroy the Environment

Modern methods of farming and agriculture give us the ability to produce _plenty of food_ for everyone. But there's a hefty _price_ to pay. One that we're already paying.
Modern Farming methods can _damage the world we live in_, making it _polluted_, _unattractive_ and _bereft of wildlife_. The main effects are:

1) _REMOVAL OF HEDGES_ to make huge great fields for _maximum efficiency_.
   This _destroys the natural habitat_ of many _wild creatures_, and can lead to serious _soil erosion_.
2) Loss of meadowlands full of wild flowers, of natural woodlands and orchards of cherry trees, of rolling fields of grass and flowers, and tree-topped hills and leafy lanes — just _swept away_ in a couple of decades, along with all the natural timeless beauty of rural England.
3) Careless use of _FERTILISERS_ pollutes _rivers_ and _lakes_, making them _green, slimy and horrible_.
4) _PESTICIDES DISTURB FOOD CHAINS_ and reduce many _insect_, _bird_ and _mammal_ populations.
5) _INTENSIVE_ farming of _animals_ such as _battery-hens_, and _crated veal calves_ is simply _indecent_.

It _is_ possible to farm efficiently and still maintain a healthy and beautiful environment.
But maximum profit and efficiency will have to be compromised, if we are to make our countryside more than just one big _industrial food factory_, and also to treat our fellow creatures (many of whom we will eventually _eat_) with some basic level of _decency and respect and humanity_.

DEFORESTATION — The Four Big Problems it Causes...

We have already pretty well deforested _OUR COUNTRY_. Now many _under-developed_ countries are doing the same. However, there are _several serious environmental problems_ that can occur when they suddenly cut lots of trees down in these _tropical climates_:

1) _DECREASE IN RAINFALL_ in that area because moisture is no longer evaporating into the air from the trees.
2) _SERIOUS SOIL EROSION_ when it rains heavily because there are no roots to hold it all together.
3) _SERIOUS FLOODING_ because the soil gets washed into the rivers, silts them up, and over they flow...
4) _INCREASE IN CO_2 LEVELS_ in the atmosphere because the trees aren't there to remove it any more.

So much to learn, so little time to learn it...

More environment problems. This stuff can certainly get a bit tedious. At first it can be quite interesting, but then having to make sure you've learnt all those drivelly little details is not. Still, there's worse things in life than a bit of revision. So _learn and enjoy_. It's the only way.

Problems Caused By Farming

Pesticides and *fertilisers* are both *artificial chemicals* which are spread onto farm land in *massive quantities* every year. The *damaging effects* of this haven't always been spotted straight away.

Pesticides Disturb Food Chains

1) *Pesticides* are sprayed onto *most crops* to *kill* the various *insects* that can *damage* the crops.
2) Unfortunately, they *also kill* lots of *harmless insects* such as *bees* and *beetles*.
3) This can cause *a shortage of food* for many *insect-eating birds*.
4) *Pesticides* tend to be *poisonous* and there's always the danger of the poison *passing on* to *other animals* (as well as *humans*).

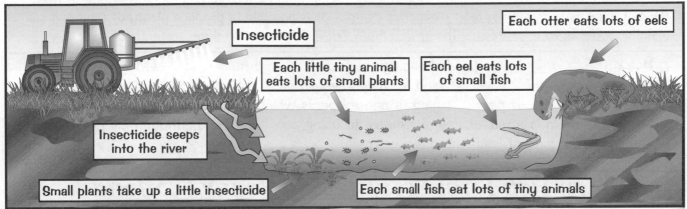

Insecticide

Each otter eats lots of eels

Each little tiny animal eats lots of small plants

Each eel eats lots of small fish

Insecticide seeps into the river

Small plants take up a little insecticide

Each small fish eat lots of tiny animals

This is well illustrated by the case of *otters* which were almost *wiped out* over much of crop-dominated Southern England by a pesticide called *DDT* in the early 1960s. The diagram shows the *food chain* which ends with the *otter*. *DDT* is *not excreted* so it *accumulates* along the *food chain* and the *otter* ends up with *all the DDT* collected by all the other animals.

Fertilisers Damage Lakes and Rivers — Eutrophication

1) *Fertilisers* which contain *nitrates* are essential to *modern farming*.
2) Without them *crops wouldn't grow* nearly so well, and *food yields* would be *well down*.
3) This is because the crops *take nitrates out of the soil* and these nitrates need to be *replaced*.
4) The *problems* start if some of the *rich fertiliser* finds its way into *rivers and streams*.
5) This happens *quite easily* if *too much fertiliser* is applied, *especially if it rains* soon afterwards.
6) The result is *EUTROPHICATION*, which basically means "*too much of a good thing*".
   (*Raw sewage* pumped into rivers can cause the same problem.)

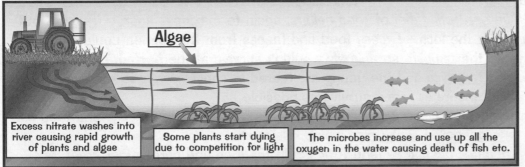

Algae

Excess nitrate washes into river causing rapid growth of plants and algae

Some plants start dying due to competition for light

The microbes increase and use up all the oxygen in the water causing death of fish etc.

As the picture shows, *too many nitrates* in the water cause a sequence of "*mega-growth*", "*mega-death*" and "*mega-decay*" involving most of the *plant and animal life* in the water.

7) *Farmers* need to take *a lot more care* when spreading *artificial fertilisers*.

There's nowt wrong wi' just spreading muck on it...

Make sure you distinguish between *pesticides* (which kill bugs) and *fertilisers* (which supply nutrients to the plants). They can both cause harm but for totally different reasons. You have to learn the details carefully. *Mini-essay* time again I'd say. *Cover the page and scribble...*

Managed Ecosystems

Organic Farming is still perfectly Viable

Modern farming produces a lot of _top quality food_ and we all appreciate it on the supermarket shelves. However, you certainly could _NOT_ describe modern farming as "_a carefully managed ecosystem_" and each _new modern farming technique_ tends to create various "_unforeseen_" or "_unfore-cared-about_" consequences.

Traditional farming methods do still work (amazingly!), but they produce rather _less food per acre_ and it's _a bit more expensive_ too. The positive side to it is that the _whole ecosystem_ stays _in balance_, the countryside _still looks pretty_ and the _animals_ get a _fair deal_ too.

Now that Europe is _over-producing food_ in a big way, it may be time to pay more attention to these things rather than "_maximum food yield at all costs_". It _is_ possible to produce plenty of food and still maintain a _balanced ecosystem_. The _THREE MAIN THINGS_ that can be done are:

1) Use of _organic fertilisers_ (i.e. spreading muck on it — and there's nowt wrong wi' that).
2) _Reforestation_ and "_set-aside_" land for meadows, to give _wild plants and animals_ a chance.
3) _Biological control_ of pests. Trying to control pests which damage crops with _other creatures_ which eat them is a reasonable alternative to using _pesticides_, and although it's not always quite so effective, at least there are _no harmful food chain problems_.

A Salmon Fish Farm Ecosystem in Bonny Scotland

In the 1980s when supplies of _North Sea cod_ started to _dwindle_, quotas had to be imposed to give the cod chance to _recover their numbers_. This was a case of an ecosystem _thrown out of balance_. In response to the problem, "_fish farms_" were set up to deliberately rear fish in a controlled way.

Salmon fish farms on the _West Coast of Scotland_ are the best known example:

1) The fish are kept in _cages_ in a sea-loch, to _protect_ them from _predators_ like birds and seals (and other two-legged ones) and also to _reduce their energy usage_ due to swimming about looking for food — i.e. they are _kept still_ to maximise the _energy transfer_ from _one trophic level_ to the _next_.

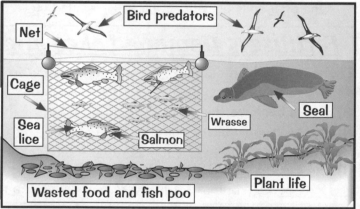

2) They're fed a _carefully controlled diet_ of _food pellets_, again to _maximise energy transfer_, but also to avoid _pollution_ to the loch. _Excess_ food and faeces from the salmon could cause _too many bacteria_ using up the _oxygen_, so _animals_ wouldn't survive at the _bottom_ of the loch.
3) The _eggs_ are _artificially fertilised_ and the young are reared in _special tanks_ to remove any risk from _predators_ and ensure as many survive as possible.
4) Fish kept in nets are more prone to _disease_ and _parasites_. One pest is _fish lice_ and they can be treated with a _chemical_ called _Dichlorvos_ which kills them.
5) However, because _chemical pesticides_ tend to _linger_ in the loch and harm _other creatures_, _biological pest control_ is used if possible. One example is the use of a small fish called the _wrasse_ which _eats fish lice_ off the backs of the salmon, thus keeping the stock _lice-free_.

Och aye the noo, wee laddie — just learn the fa'acts...

Make sure you can give a good description of a "_balanced ecosystem_" and a "_carefully managed ecosystem_", with examples. Make sure you know why organic farming represents a balanced ecosystem and why modern farming doesn't. Och aye, an' learn the fa'acts aboot fesh farms...

Managed Ecosystems

Glass House Ecosystems

Glass houses have _advantages_ for _commercial food growing_:

1) They _trap the sun's warmth_ (the _original_ Greenhouse Effect) making the plants grow _faster_ than outside.
2) They enable us to grow plants _out of season_ using _heaters_ and _artificial light_.
3) The conditions can be completely _controlled_.
4) _Carbon dioxide_, _light_ and _temperature_ levels can all be _increased_ to provide _optimum conditions_ for _photosynthesis_ and thereby _maximise growth_.
5) They can be kept _free from diseases_ and _pests_ by good _hygiene_ and _screens_.
6) _Pests_ are easy to _see_ and can be _controlled easily_ with _chemicals_ or _biological controls_.

Under-soil heaters

COMMON PESTS ARE: 1) _APHIDS_,   2) _MEALY BUGS_,   3) _WHITEFLY_,   4) _RED SPIDER MITES_

These _can_ be controlled with _chemicals_. The _disadvantages_ with _chemical pesticides_ are:
1) Some pests e.g. mealy bugs are fairly _resistant_ to pesticides.
2) The _effect_ of the pesticide _doesn't last_, so they have to be reapplied quite _frequently_.
3) They may also _kill harmless insects_ like _bees_ which help _pollination_, and also _ladybirds_ which eat pesky _greenfly_.
4) Finally, people would _prefer_ not to eat food _sprayed with chemicals_.
5) The alternative is _biological pest control_ which is pretty cool...

Biological Pest Control Can take quite a Few Months

To control pests in Glass houses there are some _special bugs_ that are just _ACE_:
1) The _APHIDOLETES_ midge lays _larvae_ which _eat aphids_.
2) There's a _special type of ladybird_ which _attacks mealy bugs_.
3) _ENCARSIA_ is a _tiny wasp_ which lays its eggs _inside whitefly_, who then get _eaten from inside_.
4) There's a _tiny red mite_ called _PHYTOSEIULUS_ which _attacks red spider mites_.
        You see, _it's all very simple_ when you know these things...

The graph shows the sort of _time scales_ that can be involved in _biological pest control_ and how the populations of _pest_ and _predator_ vary.
  Notice it can take _18 months_ (that's 1½ years) for the pesky bug to be brought _under control_.
Both populations gradually settle down to a _gentle undulating pattern_.

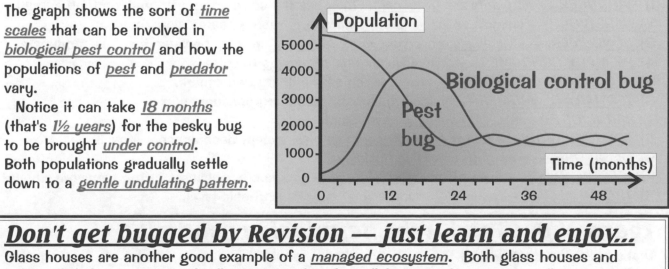

Don't get bugged by Revision — just learn and enjoy...

Glass houses are another good example of a _managed ecosystem_. Both glass houses and Salmon fish farms are specifically mentioned in the syllabuses and may very well come up in your Exam. You could do many sillier things with 20 minutes than _learn_ all these exciting facts.

Food Webs

A Woodland Food Web

Food webs are pretty easy really. Hideously easy in fact.

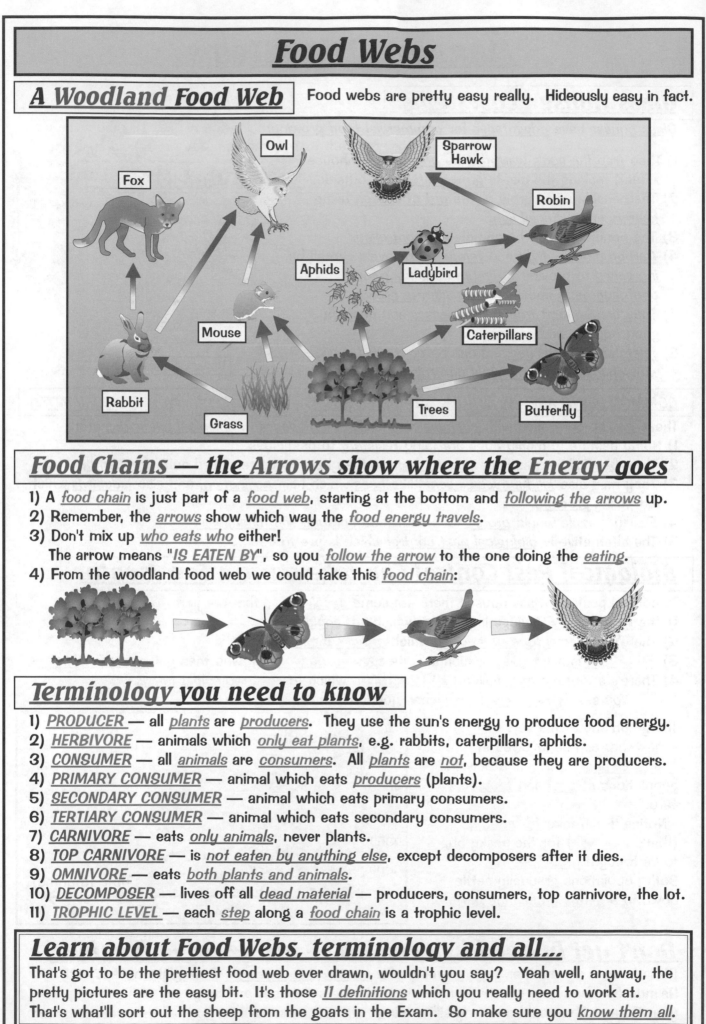

Food Chains — the Arrows show where the Energy goes

1) A _food chain_ is just part of a _food web_, starting at the bottom and _following the arrows_ up.
2) Remember, the _arrows_ show which way the _food energy travels_.
3) Don't mix up _who eats who_ either!
   The arrow means "_IS EATEN BY_", so you _follow the arrow_ to the one doing the _eating_.
4) From the woodland food web we could take this _food chain_:

Terminology you need to know

1) _PRODUCER_ — all _plants_ are _producers_. They use the sun's energy to produce food energy.
2) _HERBIVORE_ — animals which _only eat plants_, e.g. rabbits, caterpillars, aphids.
3) _CONSUMER_ — all _animals_ are _consumers_. All _plants_ are _not_, because they are producers.
4) _PRIMARY CONSUMER_ — animal which eats _producers_ (plants).
5) _SECONDARY CONSUMER_ — animal which eats primary consumers.
6) _TERTIARY CONSUMER_ — animal which eats secondary consumers.
7) _CARNIVORE_ — eats _only animals_, never plants.
8) _TOP CARNIVORE_ — is _not eaten by anything else_, except decomposers after it dies.
9) _OMNIVORE_ — eats _both plants and animals_.
10) _DECOMPOSER_ — lives off all _dead material_ — producers, consumers, top carnivore, the lot.
11) _TROPHIC LEVEL_ — each _step_ along a _food chain_ is a trophic level.

Learn about Food Webs, terminology and all...

That's got to be the prettiest food web ever drawn, wouldn't you say?   Yeah well, anyway, the pretty pictures are the easy bit. It's those _11 definitions_ which you really need to work at.
That's what'll sort out the sheep from the goats in the Exam. So make sure you _know them all_.

Making Holes in Food Webs

A Typical Food Web for a Pond

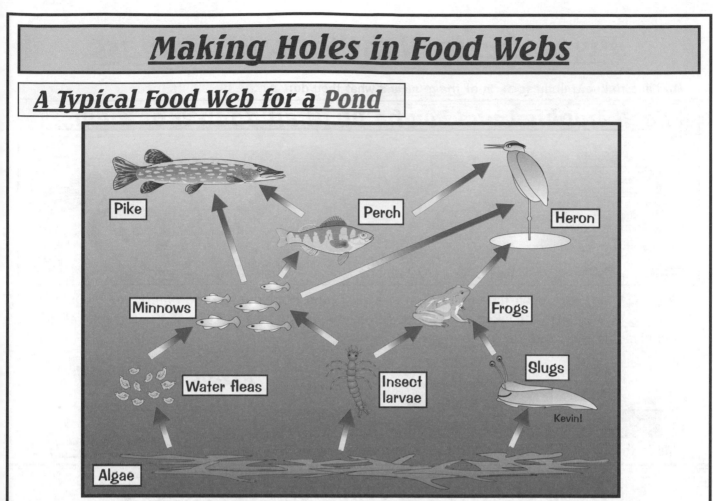

Pike

Perch

Heron

Minnows

Frogs

Water fleas

Insect larvae

Slugs

Kevin!

Algae

Exam Q. — What happens if you take out the frogs...?

1) This is the _usual Exam question_.
2) One of the animals is _wiped out_ — what effect will this have on the _other_ creatures?
3) For example, if all the _frogs_ were _removed_ what'd happen to the number of _slugs_ or _perch_?
4) It's _simple enough_, but you do have to _think it through_ fairly carefully:
   a) _SLUGS_ would _increase_ because there'd be _nothing to eat them_ now.
   b) _PERCH_ is a bit trickier. With no frogs the herons will get _hungry_ and so will _eat more perch_ (and minnows and insect larvae), so the perch will in fact _decrease_ in number.

You just have to understand the diagrams (i.e. who eats who) and think about it _real carefully_. Think about which animals _won't now get eaten_, and which animals _will go hungry_, and work out _what they'll do about it_ — and the effect that will have _on all the other things_ in the web.

Another Exam Q. — What if you took out the Minnows...?

1) First of all, _water fleas_ would _increase_.
2) _Perch_ on the other hand would be _really struggling_. They'd get _hungry_ for a start, but they'd also get _eaten_ a lot more _by pike_ and _heron_. Toughsky.
3) _Frogs_ would initially _benefit_ from _more insect larvae_ all to themselves, but would then suffer from _heron_ eating _more frogs_ due to there being _no minnows_, and then fewer perch.
4) _Slugs_ would therefore _benefit_ because the _frogs_ would be eating more _insect larvae_ (instead of slugs) and also _getting eaten_ by heron. It's all real simple if you just _think it out_.

Learn about making holes in Food webs...

If they give you a food web question you can bet your very last fruit cake they're gonna want to wipe out one of the creatures and ask you what happens then. Practise with both these food webs by wiping out organisms (only one at a time!) and deciding what'll happen to the others.

Pyramids Of Number and Biomass

This is hideously easy too. Just _make sure you know_ what _all_ the pyramids mean.

Each Trophic Level you go up, there's fewer of them...

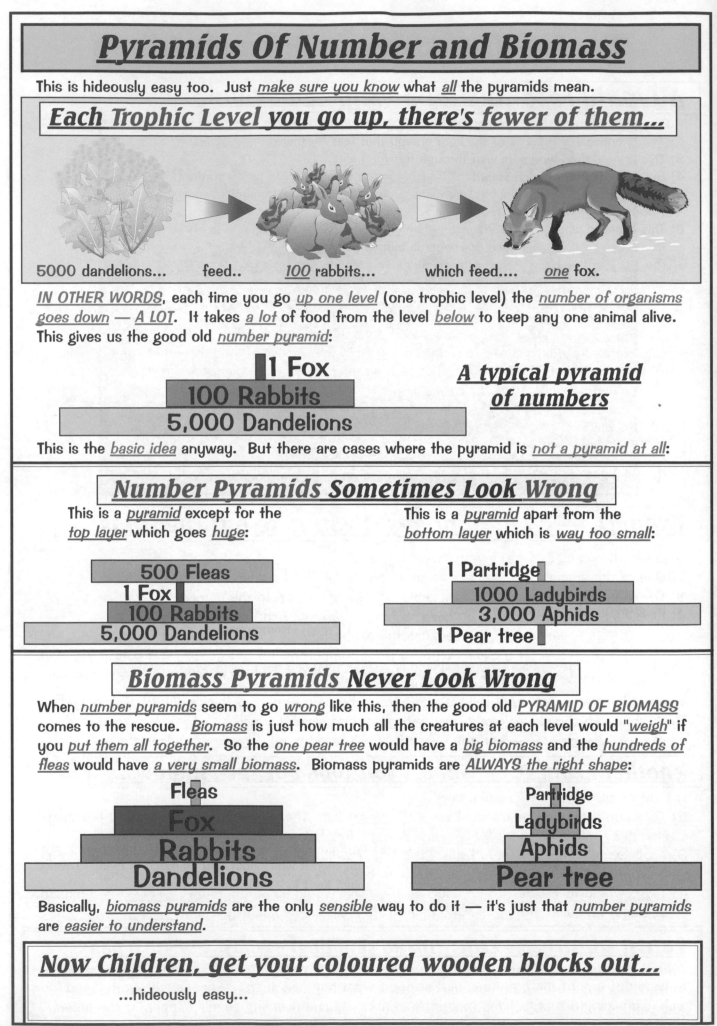

5000 dandelions...   feed..   _100_ rabbits...   which feed....   _one_ fox.

IN OTHER WORDS, each time you go _up one level_ (one trophic level) the _number of organisms goes down_ — _A LOT_. It takes _a lot_ of food from the level _below_ to keep any one animal alive. This gives us the good old _number pyramid_:

1 Fox
100 Rabbits
5,000 Dandelions

A typical pyramid of numbers

This is the _basic idea_ anyway. But there are cases where the pyramid is _not a pyramid at all_:

Number Pyramids Sometimes Look Wrong

This is a _pyramid_ except for the _top layer_ which goes _huge_:

500 Fleas
1 Fox
100 Rabbits
5,000 Dandelions

This is a _pyramid_ apart from the _bottom layer_ which is _way too small_:

1 Partridge
1000 Ladybirds
3,000 Aphids
1 Pear tree

Biomass Pyramids Never Look Wrong

When _number pyramids_ seem to go _wrong_ like this, then the good old _PYRAMID OF BIOMASS_ comes to the rescue. _Biomass_ is just how much all the creatures at each level would "_weigh_" if you _put them all together_. So the _one pear tree_ would have a _big biomass_ and the _hundreds of fleas_ would have _a very small biomass_. Biomass pyramids are _ALWAYS the right shape_:

Fleas
Fox
Rabbits
Dandelions

Partridge
Ladybirds
Aphids
Pear tree

Basically, _biomass pyramids_ are the only _sensible_ way to do it — it's just that _number pyramids_ are _easier to understand_.

Now Children, get your coloured wooden blocks out...

...hideously easy...

Energy Transfer and Efficient Food

All that Energy just Disappears Somehow...

1) Energy from the _SUN_ is the _source of energy_ for _all life on Earth_.
2) _Plants_ convert _a small %_ of the light energy that falls on them _into glucose_.
3) This _energy_ then works its way through the _food web_.
4) But _90%_ is lost at each stage. _90% of biomass_ and _90% of energy_ content.
5) So _trophic level 2_ (e.g. rabbits) contains _only 10%_ of the total chemical energy (food energy) which is stored in _trophic level 1_ (e.g. dandelions).
6) This explains why you get _biomass pyramids_. Most of the biomass from _each trophic level_ does _not_ become biomass in the _next level up_.
7) The _90%_ of the _ENERGY_ lost at each stage is used for _staying alive_, i.e. in _respiration_, which powers _all life processes_, including _movement_.
8) Most of this energy is eventually _lost to the surroundings_ as _heat_.
9) This is especially true for _mammals and birds_ which keep themselves _warm_ (i.e. are _warm-blooded_). They eat a lot more food than creatures which don't. A pet _goldfish_ is cold-blooded and only seems to need about _1/100th_ the amount of food that a pet _mouse_ needs.
10) The _90%_ of the _FOOD MATTER lost_ at each stage is passed out mostly as _faeces_.
11) Think about a rabbit. Once it's _fully grown_ it carries on eating greens but its _biomass doesn't change_, and neither does its _energy value_ to whatever finally eats it.
12) All the _biomass_ it eats must be _lost from its body_ somehow, or it would get bigger. It all goes in the _droppings_ and _urine_.
13) And once fully grown, all the _energy_ it consumes is just used for _keeping it alive_, and none of it will pass on down the food chain.
14) _Some energy_ is also lost from the food chain in the _droppings_ — they burn when dried, proving they still have chemical energy in them.

Try it next time you're camping — you'll find you enjoy your midnight sausages that much more when cooked over a blazing mound of dried sheep poo.

"Efficient" Food Production

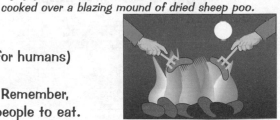

1) _For a given area of land_, you can produce _a lot more food_ (for humans) by growing _crops_ rather than by _grazing animals_.
2) This is _obvious_. You are _cutting out_ an _extra trophic level_. Remember, only _10%_ of what _beef cattle eat_ becomes _useful meat_ for people to eat.
3) In countries where good agricultural land is _scarce_, they can feed _far more people_ growing _good crops_ than by _grazing cattle or sheep_ for _meat or milk_.
4) However, don't forget that just eating _crops_ can quickly lead to _malnutrition_ through lack of essential _proteins_ and _minerals_, unless a varied enough diet is achieved.
5) Do remember also that _some land is unsuitable for growing crops_ like _moorland_ or _fellsides_. In these places, animals like _sheep_ and _deer_ are often the _best_ way to get food from the land.
6) In 'civilised' countries like ours there are attempts to improve the _efficiency_ of _energy transfer_ from _one trophic level to another_, by rearing animals like _pigs_ and _chickens_ in strict conditions of _limited movement_ and _artificial warmth_, in order to reduce their _energy losses_ to a minimum. In other words keep them _still enough_ and _hot enough_ and they won't need _feeding as much_. It's as _simple_ and as _horrible_ as that. If you deny them even the simplest of simple pleasures in their short little stay on this planet before you eat them, then it won't cost you as much in feed. Lovely.
7) But _intensively reared_ animals like chickens and pigs, kept in a little shed all their life, _still require land indirectly_ because they still need _feeding_, so land is needed to _grow_ their "feed" on. So would it be _so terrible_ to let them have a little corner of it in the sunshine somewhere, huh...?

Locked up in a little cage with no sunlight — who'd work in a bank...

Phew! Just look at all those words crammed onto one page. Geesh.... I mean blimey, it almost looks like a page from a normal science book. Almost. Anyway, there it all is, on the page, just waiting to be blended with the infinite void inside your head. _Learn and enjoy..._ and _scribble_.

SECTION FIVE — ENVIRONMENT

Decomposition and The Carbon Cycle

Another sixties pop group? Sadly not.

1) *Living things* are made of *materials* they take from the world around them.
2) When they *decompose*, ashes are returned to ashes, and dust to dust, as it were.
3) In other words *the elements they contain* are returned to the *soil* where they came from *originally*.
4) These elements are then *used by plants* to grow and the whole cycle *repeats* over and over again.

Decomposition *is carried out by Bacteria and Fungi*

1) All *plant matter* and *dead animals* are broken down and *decomposed* by *soil bacteria* and *fungi*.
2) This happens everywhere in *nature*, and also in *compost heaps* and *sewage works*.
3) All the important *elements* are thus *recycled*: *Carbon*, *Hydrogen*, *Oxygen* and *Nitrogen*.
4) The *ideal conditions* for creating *compost* are:
   a) *WARMTH*
   b) *MOISTURE*
   c) *OXYGEN (AIR)*
   d) *DECOMPOSERS* (i.e. *bacteria* and *fungi*)
   e) *ORGANIC MATTER* cut into *small pieces*.
   Make sure you *learn them* — *ALL FIVE*.

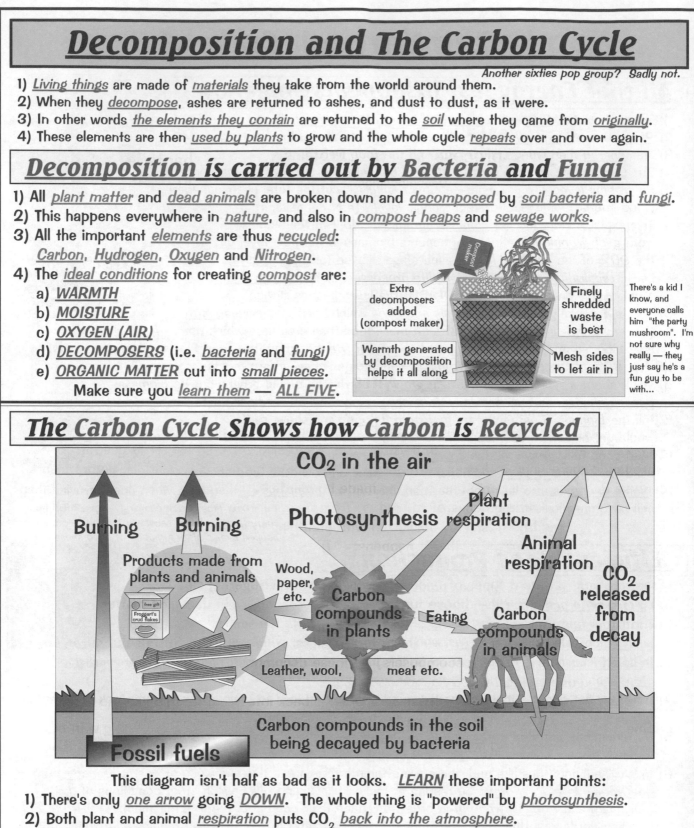

Extra decomposers added (compost maker)

Finely shredded waste is best

Warmth generated by decomposition helps it all along

Mesh sides to let air in

There's a kid I know, and everyone calls him "the party mushroom". I'm not sure why really — they just say he's a fun guy to be with...

The Carbon Cycle *Shows how Carbon is Recycled*

CO_2 in the air

Burning   Burning

Photosynthesis   Plant respiration

Animal respiration

CO_2 released from decay

Products made from plants and animals

Wood, paper, etc.

Carbon compounds in plants

Eating

Carbon compounds in animals

free gift
Froggatt's crud flakes

Leather, wool,   meat etc.

Fossil fuels

Carbon compounds in the soil being decayed by bacteria

This diagram isn't half as bad as it looks. *LEARN* these important points:

1) There's only *one arrow* going *DOWN*. The whole thing is "powered" by *photosynthesis*.
2) Both plant and animal *respiration* puts CO_2 *back into the atmosphere*.
3) *Plants* convert the carbon in CO_2 *from the air* into *fats*, *carbohydrates* and *proteins*.
4) These can then go *three ways*: *be eaten*, *decay* or be turned into *useful products* by man.
5) *Eating* transfers some of the fats, proteins and carbohydrates to *new* fats, carbohydrates and proteins *in the animal* doing the eating.
6) Ultimately these plant and animal products either *decay* or are *burned* and CO_2 *is released*.

On Ilkley Moor ba 'tat, On Ilkley Moor ba 'tat...
...where the dogs play football...

Learn the five ideal conditions for compost making. They like asking about that.
There's another version of the carbon cycle in the Chemistry Book which you really should look at, but this one is easier to understand. Practise *scribbling* it out *from memory*. And *keep trying till you can*.

The Nitrogen Cycle

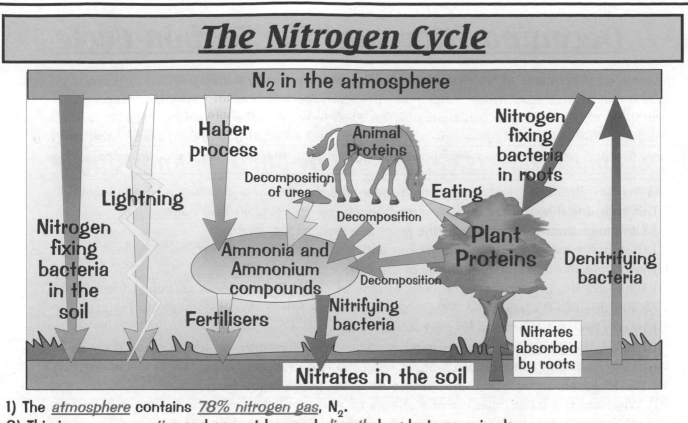

N$_2$ in the atmosphere

Haber process

Lightning

Nitrogen fixing bacteria in the soil

Nitrogen fixing bacteria in roots

Animal Proteins

Decomposition of urea

Decomposition

Eating

Plant Proteins

Denitrifying bacteria

Ammonia and Ammonium compounds

Fertilisers

Decomposition

Nitrifying bacteria

Nitrates absorbed by roots

Nitrates in the soil

1) The *atmosphere* contains *78% nitrogen gas*, N$_2$.

2) This is *very unreactive* and cannot be used *directly* by plants or animals.

3) *Nitrogen* is an *important element* in making *protein* and also *DNA*, so we really need it.

4) Nitrogen in the air has to turned into *nitrates*, NO$_3^-$, or *ammonium ions*, NH$_4^+$, before plants can use it. *Animals* can only use *proteins* made by plants.

5) *Nitrogen Fixation* is the process of turning *N$_2$ from the air* into a *more reactive form* which *plants can use* (and no it isn't an obsession with breathing in and out).

6) There are *THREE MAIN WAYS* that it happens: 1) *Lightning*,   2) *Nitrogen fixing bacteria* in roots and soil,   3) *The manufacture of artificial fertilisers* by the *Haber process*.

7) There are *four* different types of *bacteria* involved in the nitrogen cycle:
   a) *NITRIFYING BACTERIA* — these turn *ammonium compounds* in decaying matter into *useful nitrates*.
   b) *NITROGEN-FIXING BACTERIA* — these turn useless *atmospheric N$_2$* into useful *nitrates*.
   c) *PUTREFYING BACTERIA* (decomposers) — these decompose *proteins* and *urea* into *ammonia* or *ammonium compounds*.
   d) *DE-NITRIFYING BACTERIA* — these turn *nitrates* back into *N$_2$ gas*. This is of no benefit.

8) Some *nitrogen-fixing bacteria* live in the *soil*. Others live a *mutualistic relationship* with certain plants, called *legumes*, by living in *nodules* in their *roots* — the bacteria get *food* from the plant, and the plant gets *nitrogen compounds* from the bacteria — to make into *proteins*.

9) *Any organic waste*, i.e. rotting plants or dead animals or animal poo, will contain *useful nitrogen compounds* (proteins), so they all make *good fertiliser* if they're put back into the *soil*.

10) *Leguminous plants* (legumes) such as *clover* are useful in *crop rotation schemes*, where the field is *left for a year* to just grow *clover*, and then it's all simply *ploughed back into the soil*. This adds a lot of *nitrates* to the soil when the plants *decay*.

11) *Lightning* adds nitrates to the soil by *splitting up N$_2$* into nitrogen *atoms* which react with the *oxygen* in the air to form *oxides of nitrogen*. These then *dissolve in rain*, and fall to the ground where they combine with other things to form *nitrates*.

By Gum, you young 'uns have some stuff to learn...

It's really "grisly grimsdike" is the Nitrogen Cycle, I think. But the fun guys at the Exam Boards want you to know all about it, so there you go.   *Have a good time... and smile!*

Revision Summary for Section Five

There's a lot of words in Section Five. Most topics are pretty waffly with a lot of drivelly facts, and it can be real hard to learn them all. But learn them you must. You need to practise scribbling down what you can remember on each topic, and then checking back to see what you missed. These questions give you a pretty good idea of what you should know. You need to practise and practise them — till you can float through them all, like a cloud or something.

1) What are the *four* basic things which determine the size of a population of a species?
2) Sketch a graph of prey and predator populations and explain the shapes.
3) List seven survival features of the polar bear and of the camel.
4) Give five survival features for the lion and for the rabbit.
5) What are the three main sources of atmospheric pollution?
6) What are the precise environmental effects of each of these three sources of pollution?
7) What does CFC stand for? Where do CFCs come from? What damage do they do?
8) Which two gases are the biggest cause of the greenhouse effect?
9) Explain how the greenhouse effect happens. What dire consequences could there be?
10) What is causing the rise in levels of each the two problem gases. What is the solution?
11) Which gases cause acid rain? Where do these gases come from?
12) What are the three main harmful effects of acid rain? Explain exactly how fish are killed.
13) Give three ways that acid rain can be reduced.
14) What is happening to the world population? What is largely responsible for this trend?
15) What can be said about the birth rate and death rate in developing countries?
16) What problems does a rapidly increasing population create for a country?
17) What effect does more and more people have on the environment?
18) What is the great bonus of modern farming methods? What are the drawbacks?
19) What seems to be the sensible approach now, maybe?
20) List the four problems resulting from deforestation in tropical countries. Why do they do it?
21) Why are chemical pesticides used? What are the drawbacks of doing this?
22) Explain in detail how pesticides enter the food chain. What happened with DDT in the '60s?
23) What happens when too much nitrate fertiliser is put onto fields? Give full details.
24) What is the big fancy name given to this problem? How can it be avoided?
25) Explain why organic farming represents a balanced ecosystem and modern farming doesn't.
26) Describe the details of salmon fish farms in Scotland.
27) Describe the details of commercial glass houses as managed ecosystems.
28) Describe details of the biological control of pests in glass houses. Draw the graph.
29) Describe what food chains and food webs are. Give two examples of both.
30) Write down the 11 technical terms for food webs (P.86) and give a definition of each one.
31) What is the basic approach to questions which make holes in food webs?
32) What are number pyramids? Why do you generally get a pyramid of numbers?
33) Why do number pyramids sometimes go wrong, and which pyramids are always right?
34) Where does the energy in a food chain originate? What happens to the energy?
35) How much energy and biomass pass from one trophic level to the next?
36) Where does the rest go? What does this mean for farming methods where food is scarce?
37) How is this idea used to cut costs in rearing pigs and chickens in this country? Is it nice?
38) Which two organisms are responsible for the decay of organic matter?
39) What are the five ideal conditions for making compost? Draw a compost maker.
40) What is the Carbon Cycle all to do with? Draw as much of it from memory as you can.
41) What is the Nitrogen Cycle all about? Draw as much of it from memory as you can.
42) What do the four types of bacteria in the Nitrogen Cycle actually do?

Index

Index

Index

Index